GETTING BY
IN
GREEK

**A quick beginners' course for
tourists and businesspeople**

Course writer: David Hardy

Language consultant: John Pavlides

Programme presenters: Christina Coucounara
Yorgos Yannoulopoulos

Producer: Christopher Stone

BARRON'S
Woodbury, New York / London / Toronto / Sydney
By arrangement with the British Broadcasting Corporation

First U.S. Edition published in 1983 by Barron's
Educational Series, Inc.

By arrangement with the British Broadcasting
Corporation, 35 Marylebone High Street, London
W1M 4AA.

Acknowledgements
The staff and customers of Compendium Bookshop,
Plaka, Athens

All inquiries should be addressed to:
Barron's Educational Series, Inc.
113 Crossways Park Drive
Woodbury, New York 11797

Library of Congress Catalog Card No. 83-5977

International Standard Book No. 0-8120-2663-2

Library of Congress Cataloging in Publication Data
Get by in Greek.
   Getting by in Greek.
   Previously published as: Get by in Greek.
   1. Greek language, Modern—Conversation and
phrase books.   2. Greek language, Modern—
Text-books for foreign speakers—English.
I. Hardy, David.   II. Pavlides, John.   III. Title.
PA1059.G35   1983   489'.3834
83-5977

ISBN 0-8120-2663-2   AACR2

PRINTED IN THE UNITED STATES OF AMERICA

4567   550   98765432

Contents

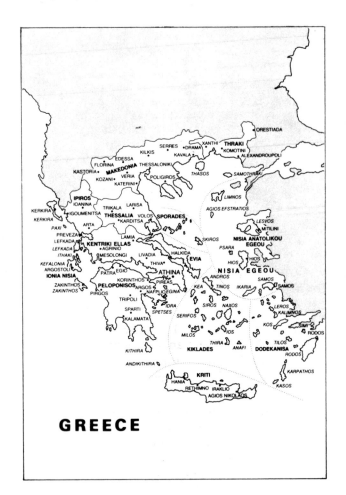

GREECE

The course...
and how to use it

Getting by in Greek is a
five-programme radio
course for anyone
planning to visit Greece
or Cyprus. It provides, in
a short learning period, a
basic 'survival kit' for
dealing with the kinds of
situation likely to arise on
a visit abroad.

The programmes

☐ are based on real-life conversations specially
recorded in Athens (Αθήνα), so that you'll get
used to hearing everyday Greek right from the
start

☐ concentrate on the language you'll need in
particular situations, such as shopping, finding
your way around, booking a hotel room,
ordering coffee, and so on

☐ help you to understand the Greek that's likely to
be said to you in these situations, and to
recognise key words and phrases, so that you
can pick out the information you need, even
when you don't understand every word

☐ give you plenty of opportunity to practise the
words and phrases you'll need to say.

The book includes

☐ the key words and phrases for each programme
☐ the texts of the conversations in the order you'll
hear them in the programmes
☐ short explanations of the language

- [ ] useful background information about Greece
- [ ] self-checking exercises to do after each programme, and a short test on the whole course at the end
- [ ] a reference section containing a guide to the pronunciation of the Greek alphabet, with a list of words to practise written both in the Greek alphabet and with English letters. This section also contains extra language notes, useful addresses, the key to the exercises and a Greek-English word list (with pronunciations)
- [ ] a list of words and phrases for use in emergencies.

The two cassettes
- [ ] contain the five radio programmes and allow you to study at your own pace. The list of words to practise in the reference section has been recorded at the end of Cassette 2, so that you can hear the sounds of Greek as you look at the alphabet.

To make the most of the course

The way you use the course will depend on you and on whether you're using the cassettes or the radio programmes, or both. Here are some suggestions:
- [ ] *The Greek alphabet:* if possible, look at the pronunciation guide on p 58 and practise saying the words in the list out loud several times. If you have the cassettes, listen to these words at the end of Cassette 2 when you practise.
- [ ] *Before each programme:* look at the key words and phrases at the beginning of each chapter. You'll find them written in English letters as well as Greek, and you should practise saying them out loud. Read through the conversations out loud several times, with someone else if

possible, and check the pronunciation and meaning of any words or phrases you don't know in the word list at the end of this book. To help you further, you'll find the alphabet written out on page 59 and across the top of each page of the word list.

☐ *During each programme:* listen to the conversations without looking at the book and concentrate on the sounds of the language. When you're asked to repeat a word or phrase, try saying it out loud, and confidently; this will help you to remember the expressions and to learn to say them with the proper stress. On the cassettes the pauses may seem a little short at first; if so, stop the tape with the pause button.

☐ *After each programme:* read through the conversations out loud again. If you have the cassettes, you may find it useful to imitate the conversations phrase by phrase, using the pause button to stop the tape. Then work through the language explanations and the exercises in the book.

☐ *When you go to Greece or Cyprus:* take this book and a phrase book with you.

1 Meeting people

Key words and phrases

To say and understand

Γειά σας Yásas	Hello or goodbye *(formal)*
Χαίρετε Hérete	Hello or goodbye *(formal)*
Γειά σου Yásoo	Hello or goodbye *(informal)*
Τί κάνετε; Ti kánete?	How are you? *(formal)*
Τί κάνεις; Ti kánis?	How are you? *(informal)*
(Πολύ) καλά ευχαριστώ (Polí) kalá efharistó	(Very) well thank you

To say

Ένα καφέ παρακαλώ 'Ena kafé parakaló	A coffee please
Ένα τσάϊ παρακαλώ 'Ena tsáï parakaló	A tea please
Μία μπύρα παρακαλώ Mía bíra parakaló	A beer please

To understand

Τί θά πάρετε; Ti tha párete?	What will you have?
Τί καφέ θέλετε; Ti kafé thélete?	What sort of coffee do you want?

Conversations

These can be heard in the programmes and on the cassettes. Check the pronunciation and meaning of new words in the Greek-English word list (p 70).

The four conversations you'll hear right at the beginning of programme one all occur later in the course. If you want to follow them at this stage, you'll find them written out on p 48.

Helloes and goodbyes

Woman	Γειά σας.
Man	Γειά σας.
Man	Χαίρετε.
Woman	Χαίρετε.
1st woman	Γειά σου.
2nd woman	Γειά σου.
Nikos	Γειά σου Αγγελική.
Angeliki	Γειά σου Νίκο.

Good morning, good evening, goodnight, goodbye

Woman	Καλημέρα.
Man	Καλημέρα.
Man	Καλησπέρα.
Woman	Καλησπέρα.
Man	Καληνύχτα.
Woman	Καληνύχτα.
Man	Καλημέρα.
Man	Καλημέρα σας.
Woman	Καλημέρα.
Woman	Καλημέρα σας.
Man	Καλησπέρα.
Woman	Καλησπέρα.
Man	Καλησπέρα σας.
Woman	Καλησπέρα.
Woman	Καληνύχτα.

Man	Καληνύχτα.
Woman	Καληνύχτα σας.

Woman	Αντίο σας.
Woman	Αντίο.
Man	Αντίο σας.

How are you?

Mrs Smith	Καλησπέρα κύριε Παππά.
Mr Pappas	Καλησπέρα σας κυρία Σμίθ. Τί κάνετε;
Mrs Smith	Καλά ευχαριστώ. Εσείς;
Mr Pappas	Πολύ καλά ευχαριστώ.

Maria	Γειά σου Καίτη.
Katy	Γειά σου Μαρία. Τί κάνεις;
Maria	Μιά χαρά. Εσύ;
Katy	Καλά.

Ordering a coffee . . .

Waiter	Τί θά πάρετε;
Customer	Ένα καφέ παρακαλώ.
Waiter	Τί καφέ θέλετε;
Customer	Μέτριο.
Waiter	Αμέσως.

Waiter	Χαίρετε. Τί θά πάρετε;
Customer	Ένα ζεστό νές μέ γάλα παρακαλώ.*

*A hot instant coffee with milk, please

. . . or a tea

Waiter	Χαίρετε. Τί θά πάρετε;
Customer	Ένα τσάι μέ γάλα παρακαλώ.
Waiter	Αμέσως.
Waiter	Χαίρετε. Τί θά πάρετε;
Customer	Ένα τσάι μέ λεμόνι.
Waiter	Αμέσως.

. . . or a beer

Waiter	Τί θά πάρετε;
Customer	Μιά μπύρα παρακαλώ.
Waiter	Μικρή ή μεγάλη;
Customer	Μικρή.
Waiter	Αμέσως.

Explanations

Saying hello and goodbye

γειά σας or **χαίρετε** – you can use either expression at any time of day, to mean either 'hello' or 'goodbye', when addressing one person rather formally, or when speaking to more than one person

γειά σου is the informal version of **γειά σας**, used when you're speaking to just one person

καλημέρα and **καλημέρα σας** literally 'good day', are used like the English 'good morning', until lunch time. During the afternoon, use **χαίρετε**.

καλησπέρα and **καλησπέρα σας** 'good evening' (from about 5.30 onwards)

καληνύχτα and **καληνύχτα σας** 'goodnight'

αντίο and **αντίο σας** 'goodbye' – at any time of day

Adding **σας** makes all the above slightly more formal.

Please and thank you

ευχαριστώ is 'thank you'
παρακαλώ is 'please'. Also 'not at all', 'don't mention it', as a reply to ευχαριστώ.

Gestures

Greeks use many facial and hand gestures to communicate without actually speaking. You should look out especially for the gesture meaning 'no': the head is tilted upwards and backwards, though this is often reduced to a raising of the eyebrows. For 'yes' the head is tilted downwards and to one side. When the head is shaken from side to side, rather like the English 'no' gesture, this implies a question: this gesture is often accompanied by a rotating of the hand, with thumb and first two fingers extended.

How to address people

κύριε to a man
κυρία to a married or older woman
δεσποινίς to a younger woman

If a Greek name ends in ς, this is usually left off when you speak to the person directly.
Γιώργος becomes Γιώργο, Νίκος becomes Νίκο, etc.

Saying how you are

Τί κάνετε; and τί κάνεις; 'how are you?'

Τί κάνετε; is the formal way to ask, and τί κάνεις; the informal. People will often move quickly to using the informal τί κάνεις; but you should use the formal τί κάνετε; with someone you are meeting for the first time.

Εσείς; and εσύ; '(and) you?' Εσείς is formal – a response to τί κάνετε; and εσύ is the reply to the informal τί κάνεις;

Πολύ καλά ευχαριστώ 'very well thank you'

Μιά χαρά 'fine' – a less formal reply, often used between friends

Ordering coffee, tea, etc

Τί θά πάρετε; 'what will you have?' Other expressions waiters use frequently are τί θέλετε; 'what do you want?' and παρακαλώ; '(yes) please?'

καφέ is the general word for coffee. If you're ordering Greek coffee, you'll need to ask for ένα σκέτο (a coffee without sugar), ένα μέτριο (a medium coffee) or ένα γλυκό (a sweet coffee).

Τί μπύρα θέλετε; Μικρή ή μεγάλη; Notice the pattern τί . . . θέλετε; 'what (kind of) . . . do you want?' The choice here is μικρή ή μεγάλη; 'small or large?'

αμέσως 'immediately', 'right away' – it's what waiters will say once they've taken your order or to let you know you've caught their eye.

Masculine, feminine and neuter

In Greek, words for things are divided into three groups – masculine, feminine and neuter. When you're ordering anything or saying what you want, the word for 'a', or 'one' is μία if you're talking about a feminine word, and ένα if it's a masculine or a neuter word: so it's μία μπύρα but ένα καφέ and ένα ούζο. See the reference section on p 62 for more about masculine, feminine and neuter words.

Accents

When Greek words are written in small letters, they have an accent on the part of the word to be stressed. Traditionally there are three accent signs ´ ` ^ but they all have the same effect and it has now been decided to use just a single accent. In this book, the single accent ´ is used, always on the stressed part of the word. You will sometimes see two other signs above letters at the beginning of words ῾ ᾿. These do not affect the way the word is pronounced, and have now been abandoned. They are not used in this book.

Numbers

0	μηδέν	1	ένα	2	δύο
3	τρία	4	τέσσερα	5	πέντε

(One is sometimes **μία,** and three and four are sometimes τρείς and τέσσερεις – see reference section p 64.)

Questions

The Greek question mark is like an English semicolon. **Τί κάνετε;** 'how are you?'

Exercises

1 Choose an appropriate greeting for each of the following situations:

i   You come down from your hotel room in the morning and say 'hello' to the receptionist:

   α Γειά σας
   β Αντίο σας
   γ Καλησπέρα
   δ Καληνύχτα σας

ii   You meet your friend Nikos by chance, and say 'hello':

   α Χαίρετε
   β Γειά σου
   γ Καλημέρα σας
   δ Καληνύχτα

iii   You go into a shop in the middle of the morning and say 'good morning' to the shopkeeper:

   α Καληνύχτα σας
   β Καλημέρα σας
   γ Καλησπέρα
   δ Αντίο σας

iv   You meet your business associate for early
evening drinks. To greet him, you say:

α Γειά σου
β Καλημέρα
γ Καλησπέρα
δ Αντίο

v   After dinner with friends, you say 'goodnight':

α Γειά σου
β Καλημέρα σας
γ Καλημέρα
δ Καληνύχτα σας

2   Practise reading these greetings out loud.

α Γειά σας
β Γειά σου
γ Χαίρετε
δ Καλημέρα
ε Καλησπέρα
ζ Καληνύχτα
η Αντίο σας

Which one would you use:
a   only in the evening...
b   only in the morning...
c   only late at night...
d   only with someone you know quite well...........
      ....

3   You're introduced to a businessman at the
hotel. How do you ask 'how are you?'

α Τί κάνετε;
β Τί κάνεις;
γ Καλά ευχαριστώ

He says he's well thank you, and asks how you are.
What do you reply?

α Καλά. Εσύ;
β Πολύ καλά ευχαριστώ
γ Τί κάνετε;

You meet someone you've met several times before who asks how you are. How do you say, 'Fine thanks, how about you?'

α Καλά ευχαριστώ
β Τί κάνετε;
γ Μιά χαρά. Εσύ;

Which of the following is he likely to answer?

α Τί κάνετε;
β Τί κάνεις;
γ Καλά

4 Choose an appropriate answer to these questions:

Τί θά πάρετε;
α Μία μπύρα παρακαλώ
β Καλά ευχαριστώ
γ Χαίρετε

Τί κάνετε;
α Καλά ευχαριστώ
β Γειά σας
γ Ένα τσάϊ μέ λεμόνι

Τί καφέ θέλετε;
α Ένα τσάϊ μέ γάλα
β Μέτριο
γ Μία μπύρα

Μικρή ή μεγάλη;
α Ένα ζεστό νές
β Ένα καφέ παρακαλώ
γ Μικρή

Τί κάνεις;
α Μιά χαρά
β Καλά ευχαριστώ. Εσείς;
γ Γειά σου

Worth knowing

Where to get a drink and a cake

You can get coffee, tea, soft drinks and alcoholic drinks, ice-cream and a cake at a ζαχαροπλαστείο, a cafe where people meet to have a leisurely chat over a drink. In summer it will invariably have tables and chairs outside on the pavement as well as inside.

You can also get a coffee or a drink at a **καφενείο**: traditionally this is a place where men meet and talk, or play cards or backgammon (**τάβλι**).

Drinks and snacks are also served at a **ΣΝΑΚ ΜΠΑΡ** or a **ΜΠΥΡΑΡΙΑ**.

As for tipping, it's common to leave a few drachmas for the waiter.

Greek coffee is very strong and served in small cups. The sugar is added before it is made, and you have to order it sweet, medium, or without sugar. You can also get instant coffee anywhere in Greece, and some places will serve French, Italian or American coffee.

Tea is often served in a pot with a jug of milk (if you've asked for it) and sugar. Occasionally, your tea may come ready-poured.

A large beer is about half a litre, and a small beer about a third.

Drinks, cakes and ice-creams

coffee
  ένα καφέ *black coffee*
  ένα σκέτο *a Greek coffee without sugar*
  ένα μέτριο *a medium Greek coffee*
  ένα γλυκό *a sweet Greek coffee*
  ένα νές *instant coffee*
  ένα φραπέ *iced coffee, shaken and sipped through a straw*
  ένα εσπρέσσο *an espresso*
  ένα καπουτσίνο *a capuccino*
  ένα γαλλικό καφέ *a French coffee*
  ένα αμερικάνικο καφέ *an American coffee*

tea	ένα τσάϊ μέ γάλα *a tea with milk* ένα τσάϊ μέ λεμόνι *a tea with lemon*
soft drinks	μία πορτοκαλάδα *an orangeade* μία λεμονάδα *a lemonade* μία κόκα κόλα *a cola* ένα χυμό πορτοκάλι *an orange juice* ένα χυμό λεμόνι *a lemon juice* μία γρανίτα *a sorbet*
alcoholic drinks	μία μπύρα *a beer* ένα ούζο *an ouzo* ένα κονιάκ *a brandy*
cakes	μία πάστα *a cake* ένα μπακλαβά *a pastry with nuts and honey*
ice-cream	ένα παγωτό *an ice-cream* κρέμα *plain* σοκολάτα *chocolate* παρφέ *mixed* σικάγο *often chocolate and plain ice-cream, with cream and chocolate sauce*

2 Going shopping

Key words and phrases

To say

Ἕνα μπουκάλι ρετσίνα παρακαλῶ
'Ena boukáli retsína parakaló

A bottle of retsina please

Μήπως ἔχετε αυγά;
Mípos éhete avgá?

Do you have any eggs?

Μισόκιλο ντομάτες
Misókilo domátes

Half a kilo of tomatoes

Ἕνα τέταρτο
'Ena tétarto

A quarter of a kilo

Πόσο κάνει;
Póso káni?

How much does it cost?

Πόσο κάνουνε;
Póso kánoone?

How much do they cost?

To understand

Τί θέλετε;
Ti thélete?

What do you want?

Πόσα θέλετε;
Pósa thélete?

How many do you want?

Τίποτ'ἄλλο;
Típot'állo?

Anything else?

Ὁρίστε
Oríste

Here you are

Μάλιστα
Málista

Certainly

Conversations

Ordering two beers . . .

Waiter	Τί θά πάρετε;
Customer	Δύο μπύρες παρακαλώ.
Waiter	Αμέσως.

. . . and two medium coffees

Waiter	Τί θά πάρετε;
Customer	Δύο καφέδες παρακαλώ.
Waiter	Τί καφέδες θέλετε;
Customer	Μέτριους.
Waiter	Αμέσως.

Buying a bottle of retsina . . .

Customer	Ένα μπουκάλι ρετσίνα παρακαλώ.
Shopkeeper	Μάλιστα.
Customer	Πόσο κάνει;
Shopkeeper	Ογδόντα δραχμές.

. . . a quarter of ham

Customer	Καλησπέρα.
Shopkeeper	Καλησπέρα. Τί θέλετε;
Customer	Ένα τέταρτο ζαμπόν.
Shopkeeper	Ναί.

. . . half a kilo of tomatoes

Customer	Μισόκιλο ντομάτες παρακαλώ.
Shopkeeper	Μάλιστα.
Customer	Πόσο κάνουνε;
Shopkeeper	Τριάντα πέντε δραχμές.
Customer	Ευχαριστώ.
Shopkeeper	Κι εγώ ευχαριστώ.

. . . a map of Athens

Customer	Μήπως έχετε χάρτες;
Girl in kiosk	Μάλιστα. Τί χάρτη θέλετε;

Customer	Τής Αθήνας παρακαλώ*.
Girl in kiosk	Ορίστε.
Customer	Πόσο κάνει;
Girl in kiosk	Πενήντα δραχμές.
Customer	Ευχαριστώ.
Girl in kiosk	Παρακαλώ.

*Of Athens please.

. . . and half a dozen eggs

Customer	Καλημέρα σας.
Shopkeeper	Καλημέρα. Τί θέλετε;
Customer	Μήπως έχετε αυγά;
Shopkeeper	Μάλιστα. Πόσα θέλετε;
Customer	Έξι.
Shopkeeper	Τίποτ' άλλο;
Customer	Όχι, ευχαριστώ.

Filling the car *(see also p 45)*

Customer	Βενζίνη παρακαλώ.
Attendant	Σούπερ ή απλή;
Customer	Σούπερ.
Attendant	Πόσο;
Customer	Πεντακόσιες δραχμές.

Explanations

Ordering more than one

When you want to ask for more than one of
anything, you usually have to change the ending of
the word. **Μπύρα** becomes **μπύρες, καφέ** becomes
καφέδες, μέτριο changes to **μέτριους, τσάι** to **τσάϊα**
and **ούζο** to **ούζα.** But some foreign words don't
change at all: **νές** and **κονιάκ** for example. The way
the word changes depends on the way it ends, and
whether it's masculine, feminine or neuter. You can
find the pattern set out on page 63 of the reference
section.

One, two, three, four and five

'One' can be either μία or ένα. 'Two' is always δύο, but three and four change, and can be either τρείς and τέσσερεις or τρία and τέσσερα. When you're ordering, or asking for things, you count μία, δύο, τρείς, τέσσερεις with feminine words, ένα, δύο, τρείς, τέσσερεις with masculine words, and ένα, δύο, τρία, τέσσερα with neuter words. All the numbers that end in one, three or four change in this way. Πέντε 'five' doesn't change. Again, the reference section on page 63 should help to make all this clear.

Numbers 1-100

1	ένα/μία	11	έντεκα		
2	δύο	12	δώδεκα	20	είκοσι
3	τρία/τρείς	13	δεκατρία/ |δεκατρείς	30	τριάντα
4	τέσσερα/ τέσσερεις !	14	δεκατέσσερα/ |δεκατέσσερεις	40	σαράντα
5	πέντε	15	δεκαπέντε	50	πενήντα
6	έξι	16	δεκαέξι	60	εξήντα
7	εφτά	17	δεκαεφτά	70	εβδομήντα
8	οχτώ	18	δεκαοχτώ	80	ογδόντα
9	εννιά	19	δεκαεννιά	90	ενενήντα
10	δέκα			100	εκατό

(You will sometimes hear slightly different variations of some of the numbers: for example, επτά for εφτά and εννέα for εννιά.)

Up to a hundred, numbers are combined exactly as in English:

είκοσι ένα   *twenty one*
τριάντα τρία   *thirty three*
σαράντα τέσσερα   *forty four*
πενήντα εφτά   *fifty seven*
ογδόντα δύο   *eighty two*

How many do you want?

πόσα θέλετε; is 'how many do you want?' You will

sometimes hear **πόσους θέλετε;** or **πόσες θέλετε;** instead. It depends on whether what you're asking for is masculine, feminine or neuter. **πόσο θέλετε;** is 'how much do you want?'

How much does it cost?

πόσο κάνει; is 'how much does it cost?' when you're buying a single item. It's **πόσο κάνουνε;** 'how much do they cost?' when you're paying for more than one thing (and a kilo of tomatoes, for example, is more than one thing). You'll often hear **πόσο κάνουν;** for **πόσο κάνουνε;**

The drachma

The Greek unit of currency is the **δραχμή** 'drachma', or **δραχμές** for more than one. Because **δραχμή** is a feminine word, you'll hear **μία δραχμή, τρείς δραχμές, τέσσερεις δραχμές, τριάντα μία δραχμές, πενήντα τρείς δραχμές** and so on. Often, though, people will miss off the **δραχμές** and you'll just hear a number: **τριάντα τέσσερεις, εβδομήντα τρείς,** and so on.

Saying 'yes' and 'no'

Μάλιστα and **ναί** are two common words for 'yes'. You may also hear **πώς** and **βεβαίως** or **βέβαια** 'certainly, of course'. **'Οχι** is 'no'.

In the shop

When you go into a shop, you may be asked **τί θέλετε;** 'what do you want?', **μάλιστα;** 'yes?', **παρακαλώ;** or **ορίστε;** Often, though, the shopkeeper will wait for you to speak first. **Τίποτ'άλλο;** is 'anything else?' When you've finished shopping and said **ευχαριστώ** the shopkeeper may reply **κι εγώ ευχαριστώ** 'thank *you*'.

ένα μπουκάλι ρετσίνα – there's no word for 'of' in expressions like this. You'll also ask for **μισόκιλο ντομάτες** and so on.

Exercises

1   The waiter in a **ζαχαροπλαστείο** asks for your order. Choose the correct way to order:

a two coffees   α δύο καφές
                               β δύο καφέ
                               γ δύο καφέδες

b three beers

α τρείς μπύρα
β τρείς μπύρες
γ τρία μπύρες

c four teas

α τέσσερεις τσάϊ
β τέσσερεις τσάϊες
γ τέσσερα τσάϊα

d three medium coffees

α τρείς μέτριους
β τρία μέτριους
γ τρία μέτριο

e two ouzos

α δύο ούζους
β δύο ούζο
γ δύο ούζα

2 You go into a small shop and the shopkeeper says **Καλημέρα. Τί θέλετε;** Does he mean:

a Good evening. What do you want?
b Good morning. What do you want?
c Good morning. How are you?

You want to ask for a quarter of a kilo of ham. Do you say:

α μισόκιλο ζαμπόν
β ένα τέταρτο ζαμπόν
γ ζαμπόν παρακαλώ

He gives you the ham and says **τίποτ´άλλο;** Is he saying:

a There you are
b That's 50 drachmas
c Anything else?

You want to know if he's any tomatoes. Do you say:

α μισόκιλο ντομάτες
β μήπως έχετε ντομάτες;
γ ένα τέταρτο ντομάτες

When you get the tomatoes, you want to know how much they cost. Do you say:

α Πόσο κάνουνε;
β Πόσο κάνει;
γ Τί κάνετε;

He says they're **πενήντα οχτώ δραχμές**. Is that:

a eighteen drachmas
b fifty eight drachmas
c eighty five drachmas

3 You're shopping for a picnic. Order the following items:

i half a kilo of tomatoes...
ii a quarter kilo of ham...
iii six eggs ....
iv a bottle of retsina...

Ντομάτες	80	τό κιλό
ρετσίνα	85	τό μπουκάλι
φέτα	150	τό κιλό
Κασέρι	145	τό κιλό
Ζαμπόν	120	τό κιλό
αυγά	5	

4 Look at the price list above and work out the price of each of the items you have just ordered in Exercise 3. How much do you have to pay altogether? Tomatoes and some other items are priced by the kilo.

Worth knowing

Shopping for food

There is a growing number of supermarkets in Athens and the larger towns. Look for the sign **ΣΟΥΠΕΡΜΑΡΚΕΤ** or **ΥΠΕΡΑΓΟΡΑ**. In smaller towns and villages, look for the grocer's shop with the sign **ΠΑΝΤΟΠΩΛΕΙΟΝ**.

You can buy bread (**ψωμί**) at the shop with the sign **ΑΡΤΟΠΟΙΕΙΟΝ** or **ΑΡΤΟΠΩΛΕΙΟΝ** (though when you're asking the way to the baker's you need to ask for **ο φούρνος**).

Kiosks

Περίπτερα, 'kiosks', are open much longer hours than the shops, and sell a surprisingly wide range of goods, including toilet articles such as tooth-paste, soap, disposable razors and so on.

The post office

The post office is the **ΤΑΧΥΔΡΟΜΕΙΟΝ**. The post office colour is yellow, and the abbreviation **ΕΛΤΑ** (**Ελληνικά Ταχυδρομεία** – Greek post offices) is often used.

The word for stamp is **γραμματόσημο** (**γραμματόσημα** for more than one) and if you want to buy stamps 'for the U.S.', it's **γιά τήν Αμερική**.

Telephones

You can make phone calls from many of the kiosks, or from telephone boxes with the sign **ΤΗΛΕΦΩΝΟΝ**. Boxes with this sign on a blue background are for local calls only; inter-city phones have an orange background. You can also make long distance calls, or send a telegram, from the **OTE** – the Greek telecommunications service.

The main office in central Athens is open 24 hours. Regional offices close late evening.

The chemist's

The sign for the chemist's is **ΦΑΡΜΑΚΕΙΟΝ**: many chemists will diagnose minor complaints.

For emergency first aid, you can call Athens First Aid Station at 166.

The butcher's

You can buy meat at a **ΚΡΕΟΠΩΛΕΙΟΝ**. The cuts of meat are different from those in the U.S. but, in general terms, **μοσχάρι** is veal, **χοιρινό** is pork, and **αρνάκι** is lamb. For mince, ask for **κυμά**. Sausages **λουκάνικα** are not sold at butcher's shops, but where you see the sign **ΑΛΛΑΝΤΙΚΑ**. For steak you should ask for **μπόν φιλέ**. Chops or cutlets are **μπριζόλες**.

The final **N** on many of the shop signs etc is not pronounced in everyday speech. You will *see* **ΦΑΡΜΑΚΕΙΟΝ, ΤΑΧΥΔΡΟΜΕΙΟΝ, ΕΣΤΙΑΤΟΡΙΟΝ, ΤΗΛΕΦΩΝΟΝ** but you *say* **φαρμακείο, ταχυδρομείο, εστιατόριο, τηλέφωνο**.

Weights

The basic measure of weight is the kilo – **τό κιλό**. Half a kilo is **μισόκιλο**, and a quarter is **ένα τέταρτο** (three quarters is **τρία τέταρτα**). Liquids are also sold by weight, as well as by the bottle (**τό μπουκάλι**).

3 Booking a hotel room

Key words and phrases

To say

Μήπως έχετε δωμάτια; Mípos éhete thomátia?	Do you have any rooms?
Έχω κλείσει ένα δωμάτιο 'Eho klísi éna thomátio	I've reserved a room
Ένα δίκλινο 'Ena thíklino	A double
θέλω νά χαλάσω πενήντα δολλάρια Thélo na haláso penínda dholária	I want to change fifty dollars

To understand

Τί δωμάτιο θέλετε; Tí thomátio thélete?	What room do you want?
Γιά πόσες μέρες; Ya póses méres?	For how many days?
Δυστυχώς δέν έχουμε Thistihós thén éhoome	Unfortunately we don't have
Είμαστε γεμάτοι 'Imaste yemáti	We're full
Τό όνομά σας παρακαλώ To ónomásas parakaló	Your name please
Τό διαβατήριό σας παρακαλώ To thiavatíriósas parakaló	Your passport please
Υπογράψτε παρακαλώ Ipográpste parakaló	Sign please

Conversations

Booking a double room

Tourist	Καλημέρα.
Receptionist	Καλημέρα σας.
Tourist	Μήπως έχετε δωμάτια;
Receptionist	Βεβαίως. Τί δωμάτιο θέλετε;
Tourist	Ἕνα δίκλινο.
Receptionist	Μάλιστα. Μέ μπάνιο;
Tourist	Ναί.
Receptionist	Γιά πόσες μέρες;
Tourist	Τρείς.
Receptionist	Εντάξει. Τό διαβατήριό σας παρακαλώ.
Tourist	Ορίστε.
Receptionist	Ευχαριστώ.

Finding the hotel full

Tourist	Μήπως έχετε δωμάτια;
Receptionist	Δυστυχώς δέν έχουμε.
	Είμαστε γεμάτοι.

A room booked in advance

Tourist	Καλησπέρα σας.
Receptionist	Καλησπέρα.
Tourist	Έχω κλείσει ένα δωμάτιο.
Receptionist	Τό όνομά σας παρακαλώ;
Tourist	Σμίθ.
Receptionist	Τό δωμάτιό σας είναι
	στό δεύτερο όροφο.*
Tourist	Τί αριθμό;
Receptionist	Διακόσια πέντε.
Tourist	Ευχαριστώ.
Receptionist	Παρακαλώ.

*Your room is on the second floor.

Changing traveller's cheques

Tourist	Χαλάτε traveller's cheques;
Bank clerk	Ναί. Βεβαίως.

Tourist	Θέλω νά χαλάσω πενήντα λίρες.
Bank clerk	Ευχαρίστως. Υπογράψτε παρακαλώ.
Tourist	Ορίστε.
Bank clerk	Τό διαβατήριό σας παρακαλώ.
Tourist	Ορίστε.
Bank clerk	*(Checks the tourist's passport and counts out the money.)* Ορίστε.
Tourist	Ευχαριστώ. Γειά σας.
Bank clerk	Γειά σας.

Explanations

Hotel rooms

A single room is ένα μονόκλινο, a double ένα δίκλινο and a room with three beds ένα τρίκλινο. A δίκλινο will have two beds by the way. If you want a double bed, you should ask for a room μέ διπλό κρεββάτι.

μέ μπάνιο is 'with a bath', μέ ντούς is 'with a shower'.

For how long?

γιά πόσες μέρες; 'for how many days?' You may also hear πόσο θά μείνετε; 'how long are you going to stay?', to which the answer is δύο/τρείς μέρες etc. μία εβδομάδα is 'one week'.

Numbers over 100

100	εκατό	600	εξακόσια
200	διακόσια	700	εφτακόσια
300	τριακόσια	800	οχτακόσια
400	τετρακόσια	900	εννιακόσια
500	πεντακόσια	1000	χίλια

2000	δύο χιλιάδες
3000	τρείς χιλιάδες
4000	τέσσερεις χιλιάδες, and so on

The numbers 200, 300, 400 . . . up to 1000 change their ending depending on whether the things you are counting are masculine, feminine or neuter. If you're talking about drachmas, they're feminine and it's **διακόσιες, τριακόσιες, τετρακόσιες δραχμές** up to a thousand **χίλιες**.

When these higher numbers are combined, there is no word for 'and' as there is in English.

Some prices in drachmas:

πεντακόσιες οχτώ   508
οχτακόσιες σαράντα τρείς   843
χίλιες τριακόσιες είκοσι μία   1,321
δεκατρείς χιλιάδες εφτακόσιες ενενήντα έξι   13,796

But room numbers end in **-κόσια**:
διακόσια πέντε   205
τριακόσια είκοσι   320
πεντακόσια οχτώ   508

Being told they don't have any rooms

δέν is 'not': **έχουμε δωμάτια** 'we have rooms', but **δέν έχουμε δωμάτια** 'we don't have rooms'.

Your room is . . .

στό δεύτερο όροφο 'on the second floor'. **Πρώτο** is 'first', **τρίτο** 'third', **τέταρτο** 'fourth' and **πέμπτο** 'fifth'.

Exercises

1   The conversation below is one you might have if you were trying to book a room in a hotel. The receptionist's part is written out for you. Work out your part of the conversation:

You	(hello) ....
Receptionist	Καλησπέρα σας
You	(do you have any rooms?) ....
	....
Receptionist	Βεβαίως. Τί δωμάτιο θέλετε;
You	(a single please) ....

Receptionist	Μέ μπάνιο;
You	(yes)....................
Receptionist	Γιά πόσες μέρες;
You	(four).....................
Receptionist	Εντάξει
You	(how much does it cost?)..............
Receptionist	Χίλιες διακόσιες δραχμές
You	(OK) ....
Receptionist	Τό διαβατήριό σας παρακαλώ
You	(here you are)......................
Receptionist	Ευχαριστώ

2   Read these requests for accommodation out loud. Which of them suits the groups of people listed below?

α   Ένα δίκλινο γιά τρείς μέρες
β   Ένα μονόκλινο γιά δύο μέρες
γ   Ένα τρίκλινο γιά μία μέρα
δ   Ένα δίκλινο καί ένα μονόκλινο γιά εφτά μέρες
ε   Ένα δίκλινο καί ένα τρίκλινο γιά τέσσερεις μέρες

i   *Mr and Mrs Lingris, visiting Athens for three days*
ii   *Mr Smith, in town on business for two days*
iii   *Mr and Mrs Hornsby and their 4 year old daughter Salli, staying overnight*
iv   *Mr and Mrs Brown and their 17 year old son Peter, on holiday for a week*
v   *Five friends touring Greece*

3   You've just come back to the hotel and want to ask for your key. Practise saying the following room numbers out loud.

a   205 ....
b   305 ....
c   310 ....
d   410 ....
e   507 ....

4 You want to change money at the bank.
Practise the following sentence, filling in the gap
with the amounts of money listed below:

α   θέλω νά χαλάσω (50) ....δολλάρια
β   θέλω νά χαλάσω (20) ....δολλάρια
γ   θέλω νά χαλάσω (100) ....δολλάρια
δ   θέλω νά χαλάσω (25) ....δολλάρια
ε   θέλω νά χαλάσω (40) ....δολλάρια

Worth knowing

Hotels

For detailed information on hotels, and for many
other aspects of a visit to Greece, you should
consult the Greek National Tourist Organisation
(address on p 66), which also has offices in Greece.

Hotels are classified L (luxury) and **Α, Β, Γ, Δ, Ε** (A,
B, C, D, E). At the height of the summer season
you'd be advised to book in advance. The prices
quoted are usually for the room, not per person.

You can also stay in a room in a private house,
though you will have to arrange this on the spot.
The local office of the tourist police **ΤΟΥΡΙΣΤΙΚΗ
ΑΣΤΥΝΟΜΙΑ** will give you advice on this, as on
many other situations you'll meet as a tourist.

There are a number of camping sites in Greece
offering modern facilities, some of which have
bungalow-huts as well as space for tents, caravans
and camping vans.

Banks

Banks are open Monday to Friday from 8.00 am to
1.30 pm and most will change traveller's cheques
or cash a personal cheque for up to $100 if
accompanied by the appropriate cheque card. Look
out for the sign **ΣΥΝΑΛΛΑΓΜΑ** 'exchange'.

The Greek unit of currency is the **δραχμή** sub-divided into 100 **λεπτά**, though inflation over the years has made these **λεπτά** almost worthless. (You may occasionally see a 50 **λεπτά** piece.)

Banknotes

1,000 drachmas – χιλιάρικο
  500 drachmas – πεντακοσάρικο
  100 drachmas – κατοστάρικο
   50 drachmas – πενηντάρικο

Coins

   50 drachmas – πενηντάρικο
   20 drachmas – εικοσάρικο
   10 drachmas – δεκάρικο
    5 drachmas – τάληρο
    2 drachmas – δίφραγκο
    1 drachma – φράγκο
    $\frac{1}{2}$ drachma (50 λεπτά) – πενηνταράκι

4 Finding your way around

Key words and phrases

To say

Συγγνώμη Signómi	Excuse me
Πού είναι τό μουσείο; Poo íne to moosío?	Where is the museum?
Υπάρχει ξενοδοχείο εδώ κοντά; Ipárhi xenothohío ethó kondá?	Is there a hotel nearby?
Τί ώρα φεύγει τό καράβι; Ti óra févgi to karávi?	What time does the boat leave?
Τί ώρα φτάνει; Ti óra ftáni?	What time does it arrive?
Από πού φεύγει τό λεωφορείο; Apo poo févgi to leoforío?	Where does the bus leave from?
Γιά τό Σούνιο πάει αυτό; Ya to Soónio pái aftó?	Does this go to Sounio?
Πιό αργά παρακαλώ Pyó argá parakaló	Slower please

To understand

Αριστερά, δεξιά, ευθεία Aristerá, thexiá, efthía	Left, right, straight on
Τό πρώτο στενό αριστερά Tó próto stenó aristerá	The first street on the left
Στή γωνία Stí gonía	At the corner

Conversations

Asking the way to the museum . . .

Man	Συγγνώμη. Πού είναι τό μουσείο παρακαλώ;
Girl	Τό δεύτερο στενό αριστερά καί τό πρώτο δεξιά.
Man	Ευχαριστώ.
Girl	Παρακαλώ.

. . . and Sindagma square

1st Man	Πού είναι τό Σύνταγμα παρακαλώ;
2nd Man	Θά στρίψετε αριστερά στή γωνία, καί μετά τό τρίτο στενό δεξιά.
1st Man	Πιό αργά παρακαλώ.
2nd Man	Θά στρίψετε αριστερά στή γωνία, καί μετά τό τρίτο στενό δεξιά.
1st Man	Ευχαριστώ.
2nd Man	Παρακαλώ.

Finding out if there's a hotel nearby

1st Man	Συγγνώμη. Υπάρχει ξενοδοχείο εδώ κοντά;
2nd Man	Ναί, βέβαια. Ευθεία, στό δεύτερο στενό δεξιά.
1st Man	Ευχαριστώ.
2nd Man	Παρακαλώ.

Asking about boat times

Customer	Τί ώρα φεύγει τό καράβι γιά τή Σάμο;
Travel agent	Επτάμιση τό πρωί.
Customer	Καί τί ώρα φτάνει;
Travel agent	Πέντε τό απόγευμα.
Customer	Εντάξει.

Catching the bus to Sounio

Tourist	Από πού φεύγει τό λεωφορείο γιά τό Σούνιο;

1st Man	Από τήν πλατεία Αιγύπτου*.
*From Egypt Square	
Tourist	Γιά τό Σούνιο πάει αυτό;
2nd Man	Μάλιστα.
Tourist	Τί ώρα φεύγει;
2nd Man	Σέ δέκα λεπτά περίπου.*
*In about ten minutes	
Tourist	Δύο γιά τό Σούνιο παρακαλώ.
	Πόσο κάνουνε;
Conductor	Διακόσιες εξήντα δραχμές.

Explanations

Asking the way

When you stop someone to ask them the way, you can say **συγγνώμη** or **μέ συγχωρείτε** 'excuse me', or simply **παρακαλώ**.

To ask the way to somewhere specific, you ask **πού είναι . . . . ;** followed by the name of the place you're looking for. The word for 'the' is sometimes **o**, sometimes **η** and sometimes **τό** depending on whether the word itself is masculine, feminine or neuter: **o φούρνος** 'the baker's', **η τράπεζα** 'the bank' and **τό μουσείο** 'the museum'. (See reference section, page 62.) To ask more generally if there's, say, a hotel nearby, it's **υπάρχει ξενοδοχείο εδώ κοντά;** If you wanted a bank, it would be **υπάρχει τράπεζα εδώ κοντά;**

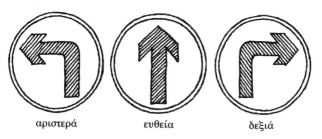

αριστερά   ευθεία   δεξιά

Understanding the reply

You probably won't understand every word of the reply, so listen out for the key words and phrases: **αριστερά, δεξιά, ευθεία** 'left, right, straight on', **στενό** 'street' (though you will also hear **δρόμος**), **στή γωνία** 'at the corner' (also 'on the corner') and **πρώτο, δεύτερο, τρίτο** 'first, second, third'.

Enquiring about public transport

Τί ώρα is 'what time?' You can ask **τί ώρα φεύγει;** 'what time does it leave?' and **τί ώρα φτάνει;** 'what time does it arrive?' **Από πού φεύγει;** is 'where does it leave from?' All three questions can be combined with the words for bus (**τό λεωφορείο**), boat (**τό καράβι**), train (**τό τραίνο**) and plane (**τό αεροπλάνο**), and you can ask **τί ώρα φεύγει τό αεροπλάνο;** or **τί ώρα φτάνει τό τραίνο;** or **από πού φεύγει τό καράβι;** and so on.

γία τή Σάμο is 'for Samos'.

To make sure that you've found the right bus, boat or whatever you can ask **γιά (τό Σούνιο) πάει αυτό;** 'does this go to (Sounio)?' (See reference section page 62.)

Clock time

The exact hours are **μία, δύο, τρείς, τέσσερεις,** and so on up to twelve o'clock which is **δώδεκα**. For the half hours, you'll sometimes hear **μία καί μισή, δύο καί μισή** 'one and a half', 'two and a half', and so on. You'll also often hear the following expressions:

1.30	μιάμιση	7.30	εφτάμιση
2.30	δυόμιση	8.30	οχτώμιση
3.30	τρεισήμιση	9.30	εννιάμιση
4.30	τεσσερεισήμιση	10.30	δέκα καί μισή★
5.30	πεντέμιση	11.30	εντεκάμιση
6.30	εξίμιση	12.30	δωδεκάμιση

★you'll rarely hear **δεκάμιση**

For minutes past the hour, it's **καί**: and so **μία καί δέκα**, **μία καί τέταρτο** and **μία καί είκοσι** are ten past one, quarter past one and twenty past one. For minutes to the hour, it's **παρά**: and so **μία παρά δέκα**, **μία παρά τέταρτο** and **μία παρά είκοσι** are ten to one, a quarter to one and twenty to one.

'At' a certain time is **στή** when the hour is one but otherwise it's **στίς**. This means it's **στή μία καί τέταρτο** 'at a quarter past one' but **στίς πέντε παρά είκοσι** 'at twenty to five'. **Σέ** is 'in' and the word for minutes is **λεπτά**: **σέ δέκα λεπτά** 'in ten minutes', **σέ μισή ώρα** 'in half an hour', **σέ ένα τέταρτο** 'in a quarter of an hour' and **σέ μία ώρα** in an hour.
On Greek timetables the initials **ΠΜ (πμ)** and **ΜΜ (μμ)** are the equivalent of AM (am) and PM (pm). **Τό πρωί** is 'in the morning' and **τό απόγευμα** 'in the afternoon/early evening'.

Exercises

1   You are at the spot marked on the map over the page. First read each of the questions out loud, and then choose which set of directions is the one that will get you where you want to go.

Questions

α   Πού είναι τό μουσείο παρακαλώ;
β   Πού είναι τό ξενοδοχείο ''Άλφα' παρακαλώ;
γ   Πού είναι τό Σύνταγμα παρακαλώ;

Directions

i   Τό δεύτερο στενό αριστερά καί τό πρώτο δεξιά
ii   Θά στρίψετε αριστερά στή γωνία, καί μετά τό δεύτερο στενό δεξιά
iii   Θά πάτε ευθεία καί θά στρίψετε στό τρίτο στενό αριστερά
iv   Ευθεία, τό τρίτο στενό δεξιά
v   Τό πρώτο στενό αριστερά καί τό πρώτο δεξιά

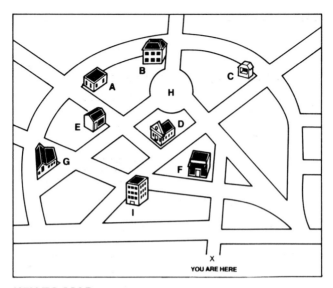

YOU ARE HERE

KEY TO MAP

A cake-shop ζαχαροπλαστείο
B bank τράπεζα
C kiosk περίπτερο
D post-office ταχυδρομείο
E chemist φαρμακείο
F taverna ταβέρνα, Ευωταδρα, τό ευωίαδρα
G museum μουσείο
H Sindagma Square τό Σύνταγμα
I Hotel Alpha ξενοδοχείο ''Αλφα'

2   Ask if there is one of the following places nearby:

i   post office (ταχυδρομείο) ....
....

ii   bank (τράπεζα) ....
....

iii   kiosk (περίπτερο) ....
....

iv   chemist's (φαρμακείο) ....
....

v ζαχαροπλαστείο.......................................
....
vi ταβέρνα.......................................

3 Match these prices with the tickets

α Τριάντα   δ Τριάντα πέντε
β Εξήντα πέντε   ε Δεκαπέντε
γ Εκατό   ζ Πενήντα

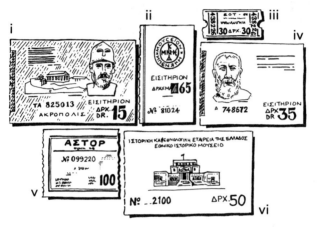

4 You want to visit the island of Rhodes by boat.
Fill in the gaps in the conversation.

You	*(what time does the boat leave for Rhodes? – γιά τή Ρόδο)*..................... ....
Travel agent	Οχτώ τό πρωί
You	*(what time does it arrive?)*............... ....
Travel agent	Τέσσερεις τό απόγευμα
You	*(OK – two please)*........................... ....
Travel agent	Μάλιστα
You	*(how much are they?)*........................ ....

Travel agent	Χίλιες τετρακόσιες δεκαπέντε
You	(Here you are)......................................
	....
Travel agent	Ευχαριστώ

Worth knowing

Getting around

By bus

There is a wide network of buses covering the whole of Greece, and there are also inter-city buses operated by the railway company (**ΟΣΕ**).

In Athens some local routes are served by trolley buses as well as ordinary buses. There is a flat fare on both. A one-man bus will have the sign **ΧΩΡΙΣ ΕΙΣΠΡΑΚΤΟΡΑ** 'no conductor' on the front; and the entrances and exits are clearly marked **ΜΟΝΟΝ ΕΙΣΟΔΟΣ** and **ΜΟΝΟΝ ΕΞΟΔΟΣ**.

By underground

Athens is also served by the ηλεκτρικός or underground. It has a single line, running from the port of Piraeus via Omonia Square to the suburb of Kifisia. Fares are cheap, and it is a convenient way of travelling between Athens and the port of Piraeus.

By boat

The Greek islands are served by boats, most of which start from Piraeus near Athens. There are four classes: πρώτη 'first', δεύτερη 'second', τουριστική 'tourist', and τρίτη 'third'.

By train

There are two rail networks, linking Athens with the Peloponnesos and the north of Greece. Neither is extensive, and buses are usually quicker.

By air

Olympic Airways operates domestic flights to many parts of Greece. The main office is in Sindagma Square in Athens.

By car

Many international car hire firms are represented in Greece and there are also numerous other companies. Bενζίνη 'petrol' is sold in litres, and there are 2 grades: σούπερ (roughly equivalent to 4 star) and απλή (2 star). The Greek motoring organisation is ΕΛΠΑ and its address is:

Odos Mesogion 2-4　　　Odos Amerikis 6
Athens　　　　　　　　　Athens
(Tel: 779-1615)　　　　　(Tel: 363-8632)

Road Assistance – Tel: 104

5 Eating out

Key words and phrases

To say

Τό κατάλογο To katálogo	The menu
Γιά ορεκτικά τί έχετε; Ya orektiká ti éhete?	What do you have for starters?
Φέρτε μας μερικούς μεζέδες Férte mas merikoós mezéthes	Bring us some hors d'oeuvres
Τό λογαριασμό To logariasmó	The bill

To understand

Τί θά φάτε; Ti tha fáte?	What will you eat?
Τί θά πιείτε; Ti tha pyíte?	What will you drink?
Καθήστε Kathíste	Take a seat

Conversations

Ordering lunch

Customer	Γειά σας.
Waiter	Χαίρετε.
Customer	Τό κατάλογο παρακαλώ.
Waiter	Αμέσως . . . Τί θά φάτε;
Customer	Ένα κοτόπουλο μέ πατάτες καί μία χωριάτικη.*

Waiter	Τί θά πιείτε;
Customer	Μισόκιλο κρασί καί νερό.
Waiter	Αμέσως.

*A chicken with potatoes and a mixed salad.

Paying the bill

Woman	Τό λογαριασμό παρακαλώ.
Waiter	Αμέσως . . . Διακόσιες είκοσι δραχμές.
Woman	Ορίστε, ευχαριστώ.
Waiter	Εγώ ευχαριστώ. Γειά σας.

Getting a toasted sandwich . . .

Snack-bar owner	Παρακαλώ;
Customer	Ένα τόστ μέ ζαμπόν καί τυρί παρακαλώ.
Snack-bar owner	Καθήστε.

. . . and a cheese pie

Snack-bar owner	Παρακαλώ;
Customer	Μία τυρόπιττα παρακαλώ.
Snack-bar owner	Θά τή φάτε εδώ, ή θά τή πάρετε μαζί σας;*
Customer	Εδώ.

*Are you going to eat it here or are you going to take it with you?

Eating in a taverna

Waiter	Τί θά φάτε;
Customer	Γιά ορεκτικά τί έχετε;
Waiter	Τζατζίκι, κολοκυθάκια, μελιτζάνες, χταποδάκι, τυροπιττάκια, σαλάτα χωριάτικη.*
Customer	Ωραία. Φέρτε μας μερικούς μεζέδες.
Waiter	Μετά τί θά φάτε;

| Customer | Μία μπριζόλα μοσχαρίσια
καί ένα σουβλάκι. |
| Waiter | Μάλιστα. |

*A yoghurt and garlic salad, courgettes, aubergines, octopus, small cheese pies, mixed salad.

The following conversations occur right at the end of programme five; they were also heard at the beginning of programme one.

Buying a cup of coffee

Waiter	Τί θά πάρετε;
Customer	Ένα καφέ παρακαλώ.
Waiter	Τί καφέ θέλετε;
Customer	Μέτριο.
Waiter	Αμέσως.

Going shopping

Customer	Ένα μπουκάλι ρετσίνα παρακαλώ.
Shopkeeper	Μάλιστα.
Customer	Πόσο κάνει;
Shopkeeper	Ογδόντα δραχμές.

Eating out

| Customer | Τό κατάλογο παρακαλώ. |
| Waiter | Αμέσως. Τί θά φάτε; |

And, finding your way around

Man	Συγγνώμη, πού είναι τό μουσείο παρακαλώ;
Girl	Τό δεύτερο στενό αριστερά καί τό πρώτο δεξιά.
Man	Ευχαριστώ.
Girl	Παρακαλώ.

Explanations

What would you like?

Τί θά πάρετε; 'what will you have?', τί θέλετε; 'what do you want?', and παρακαλώ; '(yes) please?' are expressions often used by waiters. However, listen out for two others beginning with τί θά . . . ; on the pattern of τί θά πάρετε; – they're τί θά φάτε; 'what will you eat?' and τί θά πιείτε; 'what will you drink?'

Bring us . . .

You'd normally say φέρτε μας . . . 'bring us . . . ' but you can also use μάς φέρνετε . . . ; If you were by yourself, it would be φέρτε μου . . . or μού φέρνετε . . . ; 'bring me'.

Exercises

1   Read these five orders for a quick snack out loud, and then match them with the five orders in English from the list below:

α   Ένα τόστ μέ ζαμπόν
β   Δύο τόστ μέ ζαμπόν καί τυρί
γ   Τρία σάντουϊτς μέ ζαμπόν καί τυρί
δ   Δύο τυρόπιττες
ε   Ένα σάντουϊτς μέ ζαμπόν, καί μία τυρόπιττα

a   Three ham and cheese sandwiches
b   Two cheese pies
c   A ham sandwich and a cheese pie
d   A toasted ham sandwich
e   Two toasted ham and cheese sandwiches

2   You're eating out with a friend. Work out your part of the conversation:

You   (call for the menu)............................
               ....
Waiter   Αμέσως. Τί θά φάτε;

You	(one chicken and one veal cutlet)....
	....
Waiter	Μάλιστα
You	(and a mixed salad please)...............
	....
Waiter	Τί θά πιεῖτε;
You	(half a kilo of wine . . .).....................
	....
Waiter	Αμέσως.
You	(. . . and water please).......................
	....
You	(call for the bill)
	....
Waiter	Τετρακόσιες είκοσι δραχμές
You	(The bill comes to . . . . . drachmas. As you give him the money, say, 'Here you are, thank you')................
	....
Waiter	Εγώ ευχαριστώ

3   In a taverna, the waiter offers you the choice of the following **ορεκτικά.** Have a go at reading them out loud. After that, you decide you'd like yoghurt and garlic, courgettes, and cheese pies. Tick the items you would order:

α   Τζατζίκι
β   Κολοκυθάκια
γ   Μελιτζάνες
δ   Χταποδάκι
ε   Τυροπιττάκια
ζ   Χωριάτικη σαλάτα

What else is on the list?..
....
....
....
....

4   You're in a snack bar with the family, who all
    want to try different things. Ask for:

i   A cheese pie.
ii   A toasted sandwich with ham.
iii A sandwich with ham and cheese.
iv   Two toasted sandwiches with cheese.
v   Three beers.

Worth knowing

Eating out

A **ταβέρνα** is normally open only in the evenings
and specialises in meat, and sometimes fish,
cooked over a charcoal grill, and a wide range of
hors d'oeuvres – **ορεκτικά** or **μεζέδες**. People go to a
ταβέρνα to spend the evening chatting over a slow
meal and one or two glasses of beer or wine. There
may also be singing and dancing. Usually, they will
order a number of hors d'oeuvres and spend some
time over those before proceeding to the main
dish. Sweets are limited – usually to fresh fruit. And
coffee is not usually served, since it is not a Greek
habit to drink coffee after a meal. People will either
sit on in the **ταβέρνα** after the meal, or perhaps go
on to a **ζαχαροπλαστείο** for an ice-cream or a cake.

An **εστιατόριο** is open throughout the day. Though
it, too, may have a charcoal grill (normally only
used in the evenings) it differs from the **ταβέρνα** in
having a large number of ready-cooked dishes.
Many **εστιατόρια** are particularly busy at lunch
times (2 pm-3 pm).

The **ταβέρνα** will frequently not have a menu (the
waiter will tell you what's on) though the **εστιατόριο**
probably will have one. In both it is quite common
for people to go into the kitchen to see what looks
good before they order.

Wine

You can order wine by the bottle – μπουκάλι – or the draught house wine by weight: ένα κιλό, μισόκιλο or ένα τέταρτο. A kilo is about a litre. For a single glass of wine, ask for ένα ποτήρι (water glass size) or ένα ποτηράκι (wine glass).

What's on the menu?

The menu in an εστιατόριο can seem quite complicated. Look under the heading ΕΝΤΡΑΔΕΣ for main dishes, where you'll find μοσχάρι (veal), χοιρινό (pork), αρνί or αρνάκι (lamb) and κοτόπουλο (chicken) – each with a variety of garnishes. Under ΨΗΤΑ you'll find roast dishes, and ΛΑΔΕΡΑ (dishes cooked in oil) and ΚΥΜΑΔΕΣ (dishes with mince meat) will include things like κεφτέδες (meat balls) and ντομάτες γεμιστές (stuffed tomatoes).

If you want freshly cooked food (available mainly in the evening) try the section headed ΤΗΣ ΩΡΑΣ (food cooked 'at the time').

Salads are listed under ΣΑΛΑΤΕΣ and sweets under ΓΛΥΚΑ. The most common dessert, however, is fresh fruit, found under ΦΡΟΥΤΑ.

The Greek habit is to eat much later than in the U.S. The restaurants fill up at lunch time between 2 pm and 3 pm: and in the evening, 9 pm is an early time to start – a ταβέρνα will fill up between 10 pm and 11 pm.

Snacks

One common snack in Greece is σουβλάκι μέ πίττα, chunks of grilled meat and salad wrapped in pitta bread. And there are many snack-bars where you can buy a τυρόπιττα 'cheese pie', a σπανακόπιττα 'spinach pie', a κρεατόπιττα 'meat pie', or a μπουγάτσα 'pastry filled with custard'. There are also snack-bars where you can buy a toasted sandwich (τόστ) or a plain sandwich (σάντουιτς). Both have a wide variety of fillings.

Can you 'GET BY'?

Test

Try these exercises when you've finished the course. The answers are on page 69.

1 Choose a suitable greeting from the list below for each of these situations:

i You meet Mr Pappas at a dinner party in the evening

ii You meet your friend Nikos by chance in a bookshop

iii You go into a travel agency in the middle of the morning

iv You leave a group of friends at a taverna about midnight to go back to your hotel

v You say goodbye to the hotel receptionist as you leave to catch your plane home

α Καλημέρα σας
β Καλησπέρα
γ Γειά σου
δ Αντίο σας
ε Καληνύχτα σας

2

a You meet your new colleague's wife for the first time. How do you say 'Hello, how are you?'

....

b She says **καλά ευχαριστώ, εσείς;** How do you say 'Very well thank you'? ....

....

c Now you meet her brother, who asks **Τί κάνετε;** How do you say 'I'm well thanks, how about you?' ....

....

d You meet an old friend on the boat to Samos. Say 'Hello, how are you?' ....

....

e He says **μία χαρά, εσύ;** How do you say you're well?...

f Another close friend meets you from the boat and asks **τί κάνεις;** How do you say, 'I'm fine, how are you?' ....

....

3 Read the following questions and requests out loud, and then choose the situation in which you might say them from the list below.

α Ένα σκέτο παρακαλώ
β Μήπως έχετε αυγά;
γ Μήπως έχετε δωμάτια;
δ Θέλω νά χαλάσω πενήντα λίρες
ε Πού είναι τό μουσείο παρακαλώ;
ζ Τί ώρα φεύγει τό καράβι;
η Γιά τό Σούνιο πάει αυτό;
θ Τό κατάλογο παρακαλώ;
ι Γιά ορεκτικά τί έχετε;
κ Μία τυρόπιττα παρακαλώ

i   In a hotel
ii   In the street
iii At the bus station
iv   At the **ταβέρνα**
v   In a snack-bar
vi   At a **ζαχαροπλαστείο**
vii At a grocer's
viii At a bank
ix   At a travel agency
x   In an **εστιατόριο**

4 You're in a **ζαχαροπλαστείο** and a group of friends want you to show off your Greek and do all the ordering. How do you ask for:

a a sweet coffee ....

b	an instant coffee with milk	....
		....
c	one tea with lemon	....
d	two teas with milk	....
		....
e	three beers	....
f	two medium coffees	....

5 You're out shopping. How do you ask for these items:

a	half a kilo of ham	....
b	one kilo of tomatoes	....
c	a dozen eggs	....
d	a bottle of retsina	....
		....
e	a map of Athens	....

6 You've just arrived in a small town, and you want to find a hotel and some other places nearby. How do you ask:

a	Is there a hotel nearby?	....
		....
b	Where is the museum?	....
		....
c	Where is the bank?	....
		....
d	Is there a chemist's anywhere nearby?	....
		....
e	Where is the baker's?	....
		....
f	Is there a kiosk nearby?	....
		....

7 Look at the following sets of directions. Pick out the key words, and note down the way you have to go (eg first right, second left):

α Θά πάρετε τό πρώτο στενό ἀριστερά, καί μετά θά στρίψετε στό πρώτο δεξιά ....
....

β Θά στρίψετε αριστερά στή γωνία, καί θά πάρετε τό τρίτο στενό δεξιά...
....

γ Τό δεύτερο στενό δεξιά, καί μετά τό τρίτο αριστερά..
....

δ Θά πάτε ευθεία καί θά στρίψετε αριστερά στή γωνία..

ε Θά πάρετε τό πρώτο στενό αριστερά καί μετά τό τρίτο στενό αριστερά..
....

8 Read the following prices out loud and then write down in figures how much they are:

α Πενήντα πέντε ....
β Ογδόντα τρείς..
γ Εκατόν εξήντα μία.......................................
δ Πεντακόσιες εβδομήντα εννιά.........................
ε Χίλιες διακόσιες..
ζ Τρείς χιλιάδες τετρακόσιες σαράντα ....

9 You're planning your holiday excursions. How do you ask:

a What time does the boat to Rhodes (γιά τή Ρόδο) leave?..
b What time does it arrive?..............................
c How much does it cost?................................
d What time does the bus to Sounio leave?..........
....
e What time does it arrive?..............................
f How much does it cost?................................
g Where does it leave from?............................
....
h Does this go to Rhodes? ....
....
i Does this go to Sounio?................................
....

10 Choose a suitable answer for the following
questions and requests:

i   Τί δωμάτιο θέλετε;
    α ένα μονόκλινο
    β τής Αθήνας παρακαλώ
    γ ένα ζεστό νές

ii Τί θά φάτε;
    α μία μπύρα
    β ένα σουβλάκι
    γ τρείς καφέδες

iii Τί θέλετε;
    α όχι, ευχαριστώ
    β πολύ καλά ευχαριστώ
    γ μισόκιλο ντομάτες

iv Τό όνομά σας;
    α εντάξει
    β Παππάς
    γ ορίστε

v   Τίποτ΄άλλο;
    α όχι, ευχαριστώ
    β εδώ
    γ καλημέρα σας

vi Τί θά πιείτε;
    α μία μπριζόλα μοσχαρίσια
    β μία χωριάτικη
    γ μισόκιλο κρασί

vii Τό διαβατήριό σας;
    α ορίστε
    β Παππάς
    γ τρείς

viii Πόσα θέλετε;
    α νερό παρακαλώ
    β ένα καφέ
    γ δέκα

Reference section

Language

The Greek you hear in the programme is typical of that spoken in Athens and throughout most of Greece. Although there are local dialects in a few parts of Greece you will certainly be understood everywhere when you speak the Greek you've learned, and you should have few problems getting used to the local accent. This is also true of Cyprus, which has a particularly distinct dialect.

Pronunciation guide

Hardly any of the sounds in Greek present any difficulty for the English-speaker. In this guide you'll find the alphabet written out with the name of each letter and a guide to its approximate pronunciation. In the right-hand column you'll find a number opposite each letter. This refers to a word which contains the sound in the list at the end of the alphabet section. Practise saying each word out loud, first using the English 'guide' and then looking at the Greek as you say it, to help you become familiar with the way Greek looks. You can hear all the words in the list on Cassette 2, after the end of programme five.

In this way you'll soon become familiar with the Greek alphabet, and be able to read and speak all the Greek you need.

It is not important to try to acquire a 'perfect accent': the aim is to be understood. For this it *is* important that you stress the right part of the word – and in Greek each word has a stress-mark on it (see page 61).

The alphabet

Capital letter	Small letter	Name	Approx sound	Example number
Α	α	*alfa*	f**a**ther	1
Β	β	*vita*	**v**oice	22
Γ	γ	*gama*	i ba**g** (soft 'g') ii **y**es (before 'e' and 'i')	9 23
Δ	δ	*thelta*	**th**is	29
Ε	ε	*epsilon*	t**e**n	4
Ζ	ζ	*zita*	**z**oo	13
Η	η	*ita*	f**ee**t (clipped short)	20
Θ	θ	*thita*	**th**ick	8
Ι	ι	*yota*	f**ee**t (clipped short)	7
Κ	κ	*kapa*	**k**ing	1
Λ	λ	*lamtha*	**l**ong	18
Μ	μ	*mi*	**m**an	19
Ν	ν	*ni*	**n**ot	20
Ξ	ξ	*xi*	bo**x**	31
Ο	ο	*omikron*	t**au**t (clipped short)	10
Π	π	*pi*	**p**it	28
Ρ	ρ	*ro*	**r**ed	2
Σ	σ, *ς	*sigma*	**s**it	15
Τ	τ	*taf*	**t**op	23
Υ	υ	*upsilon*	f**ee**t (clipped short)	10
Φ	φ	*fi*	**f**at	32
Χ	χ	*khi*	i lo**ch** ii **h**ue (before 'e' and 'i')	27 26

*ς is used at the end of words

| Ψ | ψ | *psi* | la**ps**e | 7 |
| Ω | ω | *omega* | t**au**t (clipped short) | 27 |

Combinations of letters

	Approx sound	Example number
αι	t**e**n	26
ει	f**ee**t (clipped short)	15
οι	f**ee**t (clipped short)	16
αυ	i **af**ter	5
	ii **av**oid	6
ευ	i **le**ft	27
	ii **ev**er	17
ου	m**oo**n	24
γγ	E**ng**land	21
γκ	**g**o	14
γχ	in**h**erent	33
μπ	i slu**mb**er	3
	ii **b**at	2
ντ	i be**nd**ing	11
	ii **d**og	25

Certain sounds can be written in more than one way: αι and ε have exactly the same sound. So do ο and ω. And η, ι, υ, ει and οι all represent the same sound.

Practice words

Don't worry about the meaning of the words at this stage (most of them occur in the early part of the course) – concentrate on how they sound and on relating the sound to the Greek letters.

1 καφέ kafé	12 κέντρο kéndro	23 γεμάτοι yemáti
2 μπύρα bíra	13 ζεστό zestó	24 μουσείο moosío
3 ζαμπόν zambón	14 γκαρσόν garsón	25 ντομάτες domátes
4 έξι éxi	15 κλειστό klistó	26 χαίρετε hérete
5 αυτό aftó	16 ανοιχτό anihtó	27 ευχαριστώ efharistó
6 αυγά avgá	17 φεύγει févgi	28 παρακαλώ parakaló
7 ψωμί psomí	18 μπουκάλι boukáli	29 δωμάτιο thomátio
8 θέλω thélo	19 λεμόνι lemóni	30 καλησπέρα kalispéra
9 γάλα gála	20 Αθήνα Athína	31 ξενοδοχείο xenothohío
10 γλυκό glikó	21 Αγγλία Anglía	32 λεωφορείο leoforío
11 πέντε pénde	22 βεβαίως vevéos	33 μέ συγχωρείτε me sinhoríte

---

Accents

Words written in small letters have an accent to show which part is stressed. Under the system recently introduced in Greece only one kind of accent mark ´ is used. If you see words written under the old system, which had three different accent marks ´ ` ^, remember that all of them simply indicate the part of the word to be stressed. The two signs ' ' at the beginning of some words have no effect on the way the word is said.

Masculine, feminine and neuter

Greek names for things and people are divided into three groups: masculine, feminine and neuter. The word for 'the' is different for each group: for masculine words it's **o**, for feminine words it's **η**, and for neuter words it's **τό**: **o φούρνος** is masculine, **η ταβέρνα** is feminine, and **τό εστιατόριο** is neuter. In the word list, **o**, **η**, or **τό** is given with the word: try to remember the two together.

γιά τό... γιά τή... When you're asking for 'the (bus) for...', it will be **γιά τή** with feminine places and **γιά τό** with masculine and neuter places. You'll sometimes hear **γιά τήν** and **γιά τόν** with feminine and masculine places (but never with neuter places) if the name of the place begins with a vowel, for example, **γιά τήν Αθήνα.**

'A' and 'an'

When you're ordering things, or asking for things, the word for 'a' or 'an' is **ένα** with masculine and neuter words – **ένα καφέ, ένα ούζο** – and **μία** with feminine words – **μία μπύρα.**

Plurals

When you're ordering more than one of anything, the ending of the word changes. The list opposite shows some of the more common changes (not all of them occur in this course). Some foreign words don't change at all: **τόστ** and **σάντουιτς** for example.

Masculine words will normally end in **ς** when you look them up in a dictionary. This is the form you use, for example, when you ask how much something costs – **πόσο κάνει ο καφές;** or **πόσο κάνει ο χάρτης;** When you want to order something, ask for something, say you want something and so on, you leave off this ς: eg **ένα καφέ παρακαλώ, θέλω ένα χάρτη**. These are the endings given in the table.

Masculine words

-ο	-ους	ένα σκέτο	δύο σκέτους
-η	-ες	ένα χάρτη	δύο χάρτες
-α	-ες	ένα άντρα	δύο άντρες

but note that it's ένα καφέ   δύο καφέδες

Feminine words

-α	-ες	μία μπύρα	δύο μπύρες
-η	-ες	μία δραχμή	δύο δραχμές

Neuter words

-ο	-α	ένα δωμάτιο	δύο δωμάτια
-α	-ατα	ένα γράμμα	δύο γράμματα
-ι	-ια	ένα καράβι	δύο καράβια

Adjectives – describing words

If you're ordering things, or saying you want things, many common adjectives end in **-ο** if the word is masculine, **-η** if it's feminine and **-ο** if it's neuter (and change to **-ους, -ες, -α** if you're wanting more than one).

Numbers

0 μηδέν	10 δέκα	
1 ένα	11 έντεκα	
2 δύο	12 δώδεκα	20 είκοσι
3 τρία	13 δεκατρία	30 τριάντα
4 τέσσερα	14 δεκατέσσερα	40 σαράντα
5 πέντε	15 δεκαπέντε	50 πενήντα
6 έξι	16 δεκαέξι	60 εξήντα
7 εφτά	17 δεκαεφτά	70 εβδομήντα
8 οχτώ	18 δεκαοχτώ	80 ογδόντα
9 εννιά	19 δεκαεννιά	90 ενενήντα

100 εκατό		600 εξακόσια
200 διακόσια		700 εφτακόσια
300 τριακόσια		800 οχτακόσια
400 τετρακόσια		900 εννιακόσια
500 πεντακόσια		

1000 χίλια
2000 δύο χιλιάδες
3000 τρείς χιλιάδες
4000 τέσσερεις χιλιάδες
10,000 δέκα χιλιάδες
100,000 εκατό χιλιάδες

One is **μία** with feminine words, and **ένα** when you're ordering masculine or neuter things. Three and four are **τρία** and **τέσσερα** with neuter words, or when you're just counting, and **τρείς** and **τέσσερεις** with masculine and feminine words. Thirteen and fourteen – **δεκατρία** and **δεκατέσσερα** – also change in this way, as well as all other numbers ending in one, three or four.

The hundreds – **διακόσια, τριακόσια** etc – become **διακόσιες, τριακόσιες** and so on, with feminine words, and one thousand – **χίλια** – becomes **χίλιες**. Since **δραχμή** is a feminine word, prices are given in this form. Numbers are combined as follows (they are given in the feminine, as though they were prices):

24	είκοσι τέσσερεις
231	διακόσιες τριάντα μία
1,763	χίλιες εφτακόσιες εξήντα τρείς
13,845	δεκατρείς χιλιάδες οχτακόσιες σαράντα πέντε

100 – **εκατό** – is **εκατόν** when the following word begins with a vowel and so it's:

εκατό δεκαέξι (116)
but εκατόν είκοσι έξι (126)

Days of the week

Κυριακή	*Sunday*
Δευτέρα	*Monday*
Τρίτη	*Tuesday*
Τετάρτη	*Wednesday*
Πέμπτη	*Thursday*
Παρασκευή	*Friday*
Σάββατο	*Saturday*

Months of the year

You will hear two forms of these:

Γεννάρης	Ιανουάριος	*January*
Φλεβάρης	Φεβρουάριος	*February*
Μάρτης	Μάρτιος	*March*
Απρίλης	Απρίλιος	*April*
Μάης	Μάιος	*May*
Ιούνης	Ιούνιος	*June*
Ιούλης	Ιούλιος	*July*
Αύγουστος	Αύγουστος	*August*
Σεπτέμβρης	Σεπτέμβριος	*September*
Οχτώβρης	Οκτώβριος	*October*
Νοέμβρης	Νοέμβριος	*November*
Δεκέμβρης	Δεκέμβριος	*December*

Sign language

The following signs are very common, and you will find it useful to be able to recognise them:

ΕΙΣΟΔΟΣ
ENTRANCE

ΕΞΟΔΟΣ
EXIT

ΑΝΟΙΚΤΟΝ
OPEN

ΚΛΕΙΣΤΟΝ
CLOSED

ΩΘΗΣΑΤΕ
PUSH

ΣΥΡΑΤΕ
PULL

ΑΠΑΓΟΡΕΥΕΤΑΙ	ΕΠΙΤΡΕΠΕΤΑΙ
IT IS FORBIDDEN	IT IS ALLOWED

| ΑΠΟΧΩΡΗΤΗΡΙΑ |
| ΓΥΝΑΙΚΩΝ |
| ΑΝΔΡΩΝ |

In the lift

ΣΤΑΣΙΣ	STOP
ΚΙΝΔΥΝΟΣ	DANGER
3 ος	3rd floor
2 ος	2nd floor
1 ος	1st floor*
ΗΜ=ΗΜΙΟΡΟΦΟΣ	MEZZANINE FLOOR
ΙΣ=ΙΣΟΓΕΙΟΝ	GROUND FLOOR*
ΥΠΟΓ=ΥΠΟΓΕΙΟΝ	BASEMENT

Useful addresses

Greek National Tourist Office

645 Fifth Avenue	Odos Amerikis 2
New York, N.Y. 10022	Athens
(Tel: 212-421-5777)	(Tel: 322-3111)

Cyprus Tourism Organisation

13 East 40th Street	Odos Th. Theodotou 18
New York, N.Y. 10016	PO Box 4535
(Tel: 212-686-6016)	Nikosia
	(Tel: 021 43374)

Olympic Airways

647 Fifth Avenue
New York, N.Y. 10022
(Tel: 212-838-3600)

*The 1st floor in Greece is what we refer to as the 2nd floor in the U.S. The
ground floor corresponds to the 1st floor in the U.S.

Odos Othonos 6
Sindagma Square
Athens
(Tel: 929-2444)
(Telephone
reservations:
923-2323)

Leoforos Singrou 96
Athens
(Tel: 92921)
Odos Sindagmatos 2
PO Box 46
Limassol
(Tel: 051 62145/6)

Embassies and Consulates

U.S. Embassy
Odos Vasilissis Sofias
92
Athens
(Tel: 721-2951 *or* 8401)

U.S. Consulate
59 Vasileos
Constantinou
Thessaloniki
(Tel: 266-121)

Greek Embassy
2221 Massachusetts
Ave., N.W.
Washington, D.C.
20008
(Tel: 202-667-3168/9)

Greek Consulate
2221 Massachusetts
Ave., N.W.
Washington, D.C.
20008
(Tel: 202-232-8222/3)

Main Tourist Police Office

Leoforos Singrou 7
Athens
(Tel: 923-9224)

Key to exercises

Chapter 1

1 i α, ii β, iii β, iv γ, v δ

2 a ε, b δ, c ζ, d β

3 α, β, γ, γ

4 α, α, β, γ, α

Chapter 2

1 a γ, b β, c γ, d α, e γ

2 b, β, c, β, α, b

3 i μισόκιλο ντομάτες
   ii ένα τέταρτο ζαμπόν
   iii έξι αυγά
   iv ένα μπουκάλι ρετσίνα

4 i 40 drachmas, ii 30, iii 30, iv 85: total 185

εξήντα εφτά **67**

Chapter 3

1 Γειά σας (Χαίρετε)
Μήπως έχετε δωμάτια;
Ένα μονόκλινο παρακαλώ
Ναί (Μάλιστα)
Τέσσερεις
Πόσο κάνει;
Εντάξει
Ορίστε

2 α **i**, β **ii**, γ **iii**, δ **iv**, ε **v**

3 a διακόσια πέντε
b τριακόσια πέντε
c τριακόσια δέκα
d τετρακόσια δέκα
e πεντακόσια εφτά

4 a πενήντα λίρες
b είκοσι λίρες
c εκατό λίρες
d είκοσι πέντε λίρες
e σαράντα λίρες

Chapter 4

1 α **ii**, β **v**, γ **iii**

2 i Υπάρχει ταχυδρομείο εδώ κοντά;
ii Υπάρχει τράπεζα εδώ κοντά;
iii Υπάρχει περίπτερο εδώ κοντά;
iv Υπάρχει φαρμακείο εδώ κοντά;
v Υπάρχει ζαχαροπλαστείο εδώ κοντά;
vi Υπάρχει ταβέρνα εδώ κοντά;

3 α **iii**, β **ii**, γ **v**, δ **iv**, ε **i**, ζ **vi**

4 Τί ώρα φεύγει τό καράβι γιά τή Ρόδο;
Τί ώρα φτάνει;
Εντάξει. Δύο παρακαλώ
Πόσο κάνουνε;
Ορίστε

Chapter 5

1 α **d**, β **e**, γ **a**, δ **b**, ε **c**

2 Τό κατάλογο παρακαλώ
Ένα κοτόπουλο καί μία μπριζόλα μοσχαρίσια
Καί μία χωριάτικη παρακαλώ
Μισόκιλο κρασί
Καί νερό παρακαλώ
Τό λογαριασμό παρακαλώ 420 drs
Ορίστε. Ευχαριστώ

3 α, β, ε,
γ aubergines
δ octopus
ζ mixed salad

4 i μία τυρόπιττα
ii ένα τόστ μέ ζαμπόν
iii ένα σάντουιτς μέ ζαμπόν καί τυρί
iv δύο τόστ μέ τυρί
v τρείς μπύρες

Test

1 i β, ii γ, iii a, iv ε, v δ

2 a Γειά σας (Χαίρετε). Τί κάνετε;
   b Πολύ καλά ευχαριστώ
   c Καλά ευχαριστώ. Εσείς;
   d Γειά σου. Τί κάνεις;
   e Καλά
   f Μιά χαρά. Εσύ;

3 α **vi**, β **vii**, γ **i**, δ **viii**, ε **ii**
   ζ **ix**, η **iii**, θ **x**, ι **iv**, κ **v**

4 a ένα γλυκό
   b ένα νές μέ γάλα
   c ένα τσάι μέ λεμόνι
   d δύο τσάια μέ γάλα
   e τρείς μπύρες
   f δύο μέτριους

5 a μισόκιλο ζαμπόν
   b ένα κιλό ντομάτες
   c δώδεκα αυγά
   d ένα μπουκάλι ρετσίνα
   e ένα χάρτη τής Αθήνας

6 a Υπάρχει ξενοδοχείο εδώ κοντά;
   b Πού είναι τό μουσείο;
   c Πού είναι η τράπεζα;
   d Υπάρχει φαρμακείο εδώ κοντά;
   e Πού είναι ο φούρνος;
   f Υπάρχει περίπτερο εδώ κοντά;

7 α first left, first right
   β left at corner, third right.
   γ second right, third left
   δ straight on, left at corner
   ε first left, third left.

8 α **55**, β **83**, γ **161**, δ **579**, ε **1200**, ζ **3,440**

9 a Τί ώρα φεύγει τό καράβι γιά τή Ρόδο;
   b Τί ώρα φτάνει;
   c Πόσο κάνει;
   d Τί ώρα φεύγει τό λεωφορείο γιά τό Σούνιο;
   e Τί ώρα φτάνει;
   f Πόσο κάνει;
   g Από πού φεύγει;
   h Γιά τή Ρόδο πάει αυτό;
   i Γιά τό Σούνιο πάει αυτό;

10 i a, ii β, iii γ, iv β, v a, vi γ, vii a, viii γ

ΑΒΓΔΕΖΗΘΙΚΛΜΝΞΟΠΡΣΤΥΦΧΨΩ
α β γ δ ε ζ η θ ι κ λ μ ν ξ ο π ρ σ τ υ φ χ ψ ω

Word list

This word list gives the meaning of each word and also a pronunciation guide in English letters. It includes all the words used in this book. Adjectives are given in the form in which they appear in the course: this sometimes means they are given more than once. Shop signs etc. that appear in capital letters in the book are listed here in capital letters, and some words appear both with capitals and with small letters.

The Greek alphabet is printed across the top of each page so that you can refer to it when checking words.

Α α

η Αγγλία *England* (Anglía)
η Αγγλίδα *Englishwoman* (Anglítha)
  Αγγλικά *English (language)* (Angliká)
ο 'Αγγλος *Englishman* ('Anglos)
τό αεροπλάνο *plane* (aëropláno)
η Αθήνα *Athens* (Athína)
  ΑΛΛΑΝΤΙΚΑ *SAUSAGE SHOP* (allandiká)
  αμέσως *right away* (amésos)
η Αμερικανίδα *American woman* (Amerikanítha)
  Αμερικάνικα *American (language)* (Amerikánika)
  αμερικάνικο *American (coffee)* (amerikániko)
ο Αμερικάνος *American man* (Amerikános)
η Αμερική *America* (Amerikí)
  ΑΝΔΡΩΝ *MEN'S TOILETS* (andrón)
  ΑΝΟΙΚΤΟΝ *OPEN* (aniktón)
η άνοιξη *spring* (ánixi)
  ανοιχτό *open* (anihtó)
  αντίο (σας) *goodbye* (adío(sas))

ο άντρας *man* (ándras)
  ΑΠΑΓΟΡΕΥΕΤΑΙ *IT IS FORBIDDEN* (apagorévete)
  απλή *ordinary (petrol)* (aplí)
  από *from* (apó)
τό απόγευμα *late afternoon/early evening* (apóyevma)
  ΑΠΟΧΩΡΗΤΗΡΙΑ *TOILETS* (apohoritíria)
ο Απρίλης *April* (Aprílis)
ο Απρίλιος *April* (Aprílios)
  αργά *slowly* (argá)
ο αριθμός *number* (arithmós)
  αριστερά *left* (aristerá)
τό αρνάκι *lamb* (arnáki)
τό αρνί *mutton* (arní)
  ΑΡΤΟΠΟΙΕΙΟΝ *BAKER'S* (artopiíon)
  ΑΡΤΟΠΩΛΕΙΟΝ *BAKER'S* (artopolíon)
η αστυνομία *police* (astinomía)
τό αυγό *egg* (avgó)
ο Αύγουστος *August* (ávgoostos)
  αύριο *tomorrow* (ávrio)
  αυτό *this, that* (aftó)

ΑΒΓΔΕΖΗΘΙΚΛΜΝΞΟΠΡΣΤΥΦΧΨΩ
αβγδεζηθικλμνξοπρστυφχψω

Β β
βέβαια *certainly, of
course* (vévea)
βεβαίως *certainly,
of course* (vevéos)
η βενζίνη *petrol* (venzíni)
η βοήθεια *help* (voíthia)
τό βράδυ *evening* (vráthi)

Γ γ
τό γάλα *milk* (gála)
η Γαλλία *France* (Gallía)
η Γαλλίδα *Frenchwoman*
(Gallítha)
Γαλλικά *French
(language)* (Galliká)
γαλλικό *French (coffee)*
(gallikó)
ο Γάλλος *Frenchman*
(Gállos)
γειά σας *hello or goodbye
(formal)* (yásas)
γειά σου *hello or goodbye
(informal)* (yásoo)
γεμάτοι *full (at the hotel)*
(yemáti)
γεμιστές *stuffed
(tomatoes)* (yemistés)
ο Γεννάρης *January*
(Yennáris)
η Γερμανία *Germany*
(Yermanía)
η Γερμανίδα *German
woman* (Yermanítha)
Γερμανικά *German
(language)* (Yermaniká)
ο Γερμανός *German man*
(Yermanós)
γιά *for, to* (ya)
ο γιατρός *doctor* (yatrós)
Γιώργος *(man's name)*
(Yórgos)
γκαρσόν! *waiter!* (garsón)
ΓΛΥΚΑ *SWEETS
on menu)* (gliká)

γλυκό *sweet (coffee)*
(glikó)
τό γράμμα *letter* (grámma)
τό γραμματόσημο *stamp*
(grammatósimo)
η γρανίτα *sorbet* (graníta)
ΓΥΝΑΙΚΩΝ *WOMEN'S
TOILETS* (yinekón)
η γωνία *corner* (gonía)

Δ δ
δέκα *ten* (théka)
δεκαέξι *sixteen* (thekaéxi)
δεκαεφτά *seventeen*
(thekaeftá)
δεκαεννιά *nineteen*
(thekaenniá)
δεκαοχτώ *eighteen*
(thekaohtó)
δεκαπέντε *fifteen*
(thekapénde)
τό δεκάρικο *ten-drachma
piece* (thekáriko)
δεκατέσσερα *fourteen (n)*
(thekatéssera)
δεκατέσσερεις *fourteen
(m, f)* (thekatésseris)
δεκατρείς *thirteen (m, f)*
(thekatrís)
δεκατρία *thirteen (n)*
(thekatría)
ο Δεκέμβρης *December*
(Thekémvris)
ο Δεκέμβριος *December*
(Thekémvrios)
δέν *not* (then)
δεξιά *right (direction)*
(thexiá)
δεσποινίς *Miss* (Thespinís)
η Δευτέρα *Monday*
(Theftéra)
δεύτερη *second (class)*
(théfteri)
δεύτερο *second (street,
floor)* (théftero)

A B Γ Δ E Z H Θ I K Λ M N Ξ O Π P Σ T Y Φ X Ψ Ω
α β γ δ ε ζ η θ ι κ λ μ ν ξ ο π ρ σ τ υ φ χ ψ ω

τό διαβατήριο *passport*
(thiavatírio)

διακόσια *two hundred*
(thiakósia)

διακόσιες *two hundred
(drachmas)* (thiakósies)

τό δίκλινο *double room*
(thíklino)

διπλό *double (bed)* (thipló)

τό δίφραγκο *two-drachma
piece* (thífrango)

η δραχμή *drachma* (thrahmí)

δύο *two* (thío)

δυόμιση *half past two*
(thiómisi)

δυστυχώς *unfortunately*
(thistihós)

δώδεκα *twelve* (thótheka)

δωδεκάμιση *half past
twelve* (thothekámisi)

τό δωμάτιο *room* (thomátio)

E ε

η εβδομάδα *week*
(evthomátha)

εβδομήντα *seventy*
(evthomínda)

εγώ *I* (egó)

εδώ *here* (ethó)

τό εικοσάρικο *twenty-
drachma piece* (ikosáriko)

είκοσι *twenty* (íkosi)

είμαστε *we are* (ímaste)

είναι *is* (íne)

ΕΙΣΟΔΟΣ *ENTRANCE*
(ísothos)

ΕΙΣΠΡΑΚΤΟΡΑ
*CONDUCTOR (see
ΧΩΡΙΣ)* (ispráktora)

εκατό *one hundred* (ekató)

η Ελλάδα *Greece* (Ellátha)

ο Έλληνας *Greek man*
('Ellinas)

η Ελληνίδα *Greek woman*
(Ellinítha)

Ελληνικά *Greek (language)*
(Elliniká)

ΕΛΠΑ *Greek Motoring
Organisation* (élpa)

ένα *a, an, one* (éna)

ενενήντα *ninety* (enenínda)

εννέα *nine* (ennéa)

εννιά *nine* (enniá)

εννιακόσια *nine hundred*
(enniakósia)

εννιακόσιες *nine hundred
(drachmas)* (enniakósies)

εννιάμιση *half past nine*
(enniámisi)

εντάξει *okay* (endáxi)

έντεκα *eleven* (éndeka)

εντεκάμιση *half past eleven*
(endekámisi)

ΕΝΤΡΑΔΕΣ *MAIN DISHES
(heading on menu)*
(entráthes)

εξακόσια *six hundred*
(exakósia)

εξακόσιες *six hundred
(drachmas)* (exakósies)

εξήντα *sixty* (exínda)

έξι *six* (éxi)

εξίμιση *half past six*
(exímisi)

ΕΞΟΔΟΣ *EXIT* (éxothos)

ΕΠΙΤΡΕΠΕΤΑΙ *IT IS
ALLOWED* (epitrépete)

επτά *seven* (eptá)

επτάμιση *half past seven*
(eptámisi)

εσείς *you (formal and
plural)* (esís)

τό εσπρέσσο *espresso*
(esprésso)

τό εστιατόριο *restaurant*
(estiatório)

ΕΣΤΙΑΤΟΡΙΟΝ
RESTAURANT
(estiatórion)

εσύ *you (informal and*

ΑΒΓΔΕΖΗΘΙΚΛΜΝΞΟΠΡΣΤΥΦΧΨΩ
αβγδεζηθικλμνξοπρστυφχψω

singular) esí
ευθεία *straight on* (efthía)
ευχαριστώ *thank you*
(efharistó)
ευχαρίστως *with pleasure*
(efharístos)
εφτά *seven* (eftá)
εφτακόσια *seven hundred*
(eftakósia)
εφτακόσιες *seven hundred
(drachmas)* (eftakósies)
εφτάμιση *half past seven*
(eftámisi)
έχασα . . . *I've lost . . .*
(éhasa)
έχετε *you have, do you
have . . .* (éhete)
έχουμε *we have* (éhoome)
έχω *I have* (ého)

Z ζ
τό ζαμπόν *ham* (zambón)
τό ζαχαροπλαστείο *patisserie*
(zaharoplastío)
ζεστό *hot (ένα ζεστό νες μέ
γαλα a hot instant coffee
with milk)* (zestó)

Η η
η *the (with f words)* (i)
ή *or* (í)
ο ηλεκτρικός *Athens
underground* (ilektrikós)
ΗΜΙΟΡΟΦΟΣ
MEZZANINE FLOOR
(imiórofos)
Ηνωμένες Πολιτείες *United
States* (Inoménes
Polities)

Θ θ
θά *indicates 'will' 'shall' eg
τί θά πάρετε;* (tha)
θέλετε *you want, do you*

want? (thélete)
θέλω *I want* (thélo)

Ι ι
ο Ιανουάριος *January*
(Yanwários)
ο Ιούλης *July* (Yoólis)
ο Ιούλιος *July* (Yoólios)
ο Ιούνης *June* (Yoónis)
ο Ιούνιος *June* (Yoónios)
η Ιρλανδέζα *Irish woman*
(Irlanthéza)
η Ιρλανδία *Ireland* (Irlanthía)
ο Ιρλανδός *Irish man*
(Irlanthós)
ίσια *straight on* (ísia)
ΙΣΟΓΕΙΟΝ *GROUND
FLOOR* (isóyion)
η Ισπανία *Spain* (Ispanía)
η Ισπανίδα *Spanish woman*
(Ispanítha)
Ισπανικά *Spanish
(language)*(Ispaniká)
ο Ισπανός *Spanish man*
(Ispanós)
η Ιταλία *Italy* (Italía)
η Ιταλίδα *Italian woman*
(Italítha)
Ιταλικά *Italian (language)*
(Italiká)
ο Ιταλός *Italian man* (Italós)

Κ κ
καθήστε *take a seat*
(kathíste)
καί *and* (ke)
καλά *well* (kalá)
καλημέρα *good morning,
good day* (kaliméra)
καληνύχτα *good night*
(kaliníhta)
καλησπέρα *good evening*
(kalispéra)
τό καλοκαίρι *summer*
(kalokéri)

ΑΒΓΔΕΖΗΘΙΚΛΜΝΞΟΠΡΣΤΥΦΧΨΩ
αβγδεζηθικλμνξοπρστυφχψω

κάνει *(πόσο κάνει; how much does it cost?)* (káni)

κάνεις *(τί κάνεις; how are you?) (informal)* (kánis)

κάνετε *(τί κάνετε; how are you?) (formal)* (kánete)

κάνουν/κάνουνε *(πόσο κάνουνε; how much do they cost?)* (kánoon/kánoone)

τό καπουτσίνο *capuccino* (kapootsíno)

τό καράβι *boat* (karávi)

τό κασέρι *kind of cheese* (kaséri)

δέν κατάλαβα *I don't understand* (then katálava)

ο κατάλογος *menu, list* (katálogos)

τό κατοστάρικο *hundred-drachma note* (katostáriko)

τό καφενείο *cafe* (kafenío)

ο καφές *coffee* (kafés)

τό κέντρο *centre* (kéndro)

κεφτέδες *meat balls* (keftéthes)

κι = καί *(κι εγω ευχαριστώ thank you)*

τό κιλό *kilo* (kiló)

ΚΙΝΔΥΝΟΣ *DANGER* (kínthinos)

κλείσει *(έχω κλείσει I've reserved)* (klísi)

κλειστό *closed* (klistó)

ΚΛΕΙΣΤΟΝ *CLOSED* (klistón)

κολοκυθάκια *courgettes* (kolokithákia)

τό κονιάκ *brandy* (konyák)

κοντά *near, nearby* (kondá)

τό κοτόπουλο *chicken* (kotópoolo)

τό κρασί *wine* (krasí)

η κρεατόπιττα *meat pie* (kreatópitta)

ΚΡΕΟΠΩΛΕΙΟΝ *BUTCHER'S* (kreopolíon)

τό κρεββάτι *bed* (krevváti)

κρέμα *plain ice cream* (kréma)

ΚΥΜΑΔΕΣ *DISHES WITH MINCE (on menu)* (kimáthes)

ο κυμάς *mince meat* (kimás)

η κυρία *Mrs* (kiría)

η Κυριακή *Sunday* (Kiriakí)

κύριε *Mr (when speaking directly to someone)* (kírie)

ο κύριος *Mr* (kírios)

Λ λ

ΛΑΔΕΡΑ *COOKED WITH OIL (on menu)* (latherá)

η λεμονάδα *lemonade* (lemonátha)

τό λεμόνι *lemon* (lemóni)

τό λεπτό *i minute ii 1/100th of a drachma* (leptó)

τό λεωφορείο *bus* (leoforío)

η λίρα *pound* (líra)

ο λογαριασμός *bill* (logariasmós)

τό λουκάνικο *sausage* (lookániko)

Μ μ

μαζί *(μαζί σας with you)* (mazí)

μάλιστα *certainly, yes* (málista)

ο Μάρτης *March* (Mártis)

ο Μάρτιος *March* (Mártios)

μέ *with* (me)

μέ συγχωρείτε *excuse me* (me sinhoríte)

μεζέδες *hors d'oeuvres* (mezéthes)

ΑΒΓΔΕΖΗΘΙΚΛΜΝΞΟΠΡΣΤΥΦΧΨΩ
αβγδεζηθικλμνξοπρστυφχψω

μεθαύριο *the day after
 tomorrow* (methávrio)
μείνετε *(πόσο θά μείνετε;
 how long are you
 staying?)* (mínete)
μελιτζάνες *aubergines*
 (melitzánes)
η μέρα *day* (méra)
μερικούς *some (hors
 d'oeuvres)* (merikoós)
τό μεσημέρι *the early
 afternoon* (mesiméri)
μετά *afterwards, next*
 (metá)
μέτριο *medium (coffee)*
 (métrio)
μεγάλη *large (beer)*
 (megáli)
μηδέν *zero* (mithén)
μήπως *(μήπως έχετε . . . ;
 do you have any . . . ?)*
 (mípos)
μία *a, an, one* (mía)
μιά χαρά *fine* (myá hará)
μιάμιση *half past one*
 (miámisi)
μικρή *small (beer)* (mikrí)
μιλάτε *do you speak? you
 speak* (miláte)
μισή *half (hour)* (misí)
τό μισόκιλο *half a kilo*
 (misókilo)
τό μονόκλινο *single room*
 (monóklino)
MONON *ONLY* (mónon)
τό μοσχάρι *veal* (moshári)
μοσχαρίσια *veal (cutlet)*
 (mosharísia)
ο μπακλαβάς *cake with nuts
 and honey* (baklavás)
τό μπάνιο *bath* (bánio)
τό μπόν φιλέ *steak* (bon filé)
η μπουγάτσα
 pastry (boogátsa)
τό μπουκάλι *bottle* (bookáli)

η μπριζόλα *cutlet* (brizóla)
η μπύρα *beer* (bíra)
 ΜΠΥΡΑΡΙΑ *CAFE
 SERVING BEER AND
 SNACKS* (biraría)

Ν ν
νά *(θέλω νά . . . I want to
 . . .)* (na)
ναί *yes* (ne)
τό νερό *water* (neró)
τό νές *instant coffee* (nes)
ο Νοέμβρης *November*
 (Noémvris)
ο Νοέμβριος *November*
 (Noémvrios)
τό ντούς *shower* (doós)
η νύχτα *night* (níhta)

Ξ ξ
τό ξενοδοχείο *hotel*
 (xenothohío)

Ο ο
ο *the (with m words)* (o)
ογδόντα *eighty* (ogthónda)
η οδός *street* (othós)
ο Οκτώβριος *October*
 (Októvrios)
τό όνομα *name (τό όνομά σας
 παρακαλώ your name
 please)* (ónoma)
 ορεκτικά *hors d'oeuvres*
 (orektiká)
 ορίστε i *here you are*
 ii *yes, what is it?* (oríste)
ο όροφος *floor (1st 2nd etc)*
 (órofos)
ο ΟΣΕ *the railway
 company* (osé)
ο ΟΤΕ *Greek
 telecommunications
 service* (oté)
η Ουαλλέζα *Welsh woman*
 (Wallésa)

ΑΒΓΔΕΖΗΘΙΚΛΜΝΞΟΠΡΣΤΥΦΧΨΩ
αβγδεζηθικλμνξοπρστυφχψω

η Ουαλλία *Wales* (Wallía)
ο Ουαλλός *Welsh man* (Wallós)
τό ούζο *ouzo* (oózo)
όχι *no* (óhi)
οχτακόσια *eight hundred* (ohtakósia)
οχτακόσιες *eight hundred (drachmas)* (ohtakósies)
οχτώ *eight* (ohtó)
ο Οχτώβρης *October* (Ohtóvris)
οχτώμιση *half past eight* (ohtómisi)

Π π

τό παγωτό *ice cream* (pagotó)
πάει *goes* (pái)
ΠΑΝΤΟΠΩΛΕΙΟΝ *GROCER'S* (pandopolíon)
παρακαλώ *please, don't mention it* (parakaló)
η Παρασκευή *Friday* (Paraskeví)
πάρετε *have, take* (τί θά πάρετε; *what will you have?* θά τή πάρετε μαζί σας; *will you take it with you?*) (párete)
παρφέ *mixed ice cream* (parfé)
η πάστα *cake* (pásta)
η πατάτα *potato* (patáta)
η Πέμπτη *Thursday* (Pémpti)
πέμπτο *fifth (floor)* (pémpto)
πενήντα *fifty* (peнínda)
τό πενηνταράκι *half-drachma piece* (penindaráki)
τό πενηντάρικο *fifty-drachma note, or piece* (penindáriko)
τό πεντακοσάρικο *five-hundred drachma note* (pendakosáriko)

πεντέμιση *half past hundred* (pendakósia)
πεντακόσιες *five hundred (drachmas)* (pendakósies)
πέντε *five* (pénde)
πεντέμιση *half past five* (pendémisi)
περίπου *about, roughly* (perípoo)
τό περίπτερο *kiosk* (períptero)
πέρσι *last year* (pérsi)
πιείτε *(τί θά πιείτε; what will you drink?)* (pyíte)
πιό *more* (pyó)
η πιτσαρία *pizzeria* (pitsaría)
η πλατεία *square (eg Πλατεία Αιγύπτου Egypt Square)* (platía)
πολύ *very, much* (polí)
η πορτοκαλάδα *orangeade* (portokalátha)
τό πορτοκάλι *orange* (portokáli)
πόσα *how many* (pósa)
πόσες *how many* (póses)
πόσο *how much* (póso)
πόσους *how many* (pósoos)
τό ποτηράκι *wine glass* (potiráki)
τό ποτήρι *water glass* (potíri)
πού *where* (poó)
πρόσεξε *look out* (prósexe)
προσοχή *be careful* (prosohí)
προχτές *the day before yesterday* (prohtés)
τό πρωί *morning* (proí)
πρώτη *first (class)* (próti)
πρώτο *first (street, floor)* (próto)
πώς *yes* (pos)

Ρ ρ

η ρετσίνα *resinated wine*

ΑΒΓΔΕΖΗΘΙΚΛΜΝΞΟΠΡΣΤΥΦΧΨΩ
αβγδεζηθικλμνξοπρστυφχψω

(retsína)
η Ρωσσία *Russia* (Rossía)
η Ρωσσίδα *Russian woman*
(Rossítha)
Ρωσσικά *Russian*
(language) (Rossiká)
ο Ρώσσος *Russian man*
(Rossos)

Σ σ (ς)
τό Σάββατο *Saturday*
(Sávvato)
η σαλάτα *salad* (saláta)
ΣΑΛΑΤΕΣ *SALADS*
(heading on menu)
(salátes)
τό σάντουιτς *sandwich*
σαράντα *forty* (saránda)
σας *your (also added to*
καλημέρα *etc to make*
them more formal) (sas)
σέ *in, at, to* (se)
ο Σεπτέμβρης *September*
(Septémvris)
ο Σεπτέμβριος *September*
(Septémvrios)
σήμερα *today* (símera)
σικάγο *kind of ice cream*
(sikágo)
σκέτο *without (coffee*
without sugar) (skéto)
η Σκωτία *Scotland* (Skotía)
η Σκωτσέζα *Scotswoman*
(Skotséza)
ο Σκωτσέζος *Scotsman*
(Skotsézos)
ΣΝΑΚ ΜΠΑΡ *SNACK*
BAR (snack bar)
σοκολάτα *chocolate*
(also chocolate ice
cream)
(sokoláta)
τό σουβλάκι *meat grilled on a*
skewer (soovláki)
σούπερ *super (petrol)*

(soóper)
ΣΟΥΠΕΡΜΑΡΚΕΤ
SUPERMARKET
(soopermárket)
η σπανακόπιττα *spinach pie*
(spanakópitta)
ΣΤΑΣΙΣ i *STOP (in lift)* ii
BUS STOP (stásis)
τό στενό *side street* (stenó)
στρίψετε *(θά στρίψετε . . .*
you turn . . .) (strípsete)
συγγνώμη *excuse me*
(signómi)
μέ συγχωρείτε *excuse me*
(me sinhoríte)
ΣΥΝΑΛΛΑΓΜΑ
EXCHANGE (sinállagma)
τό Σύνταγμα *Sindagma*
Square (Síndagma)
ΣΥΡΑΤΕ *PULL* (sírate)

Τ τ
η ταβέρνα *taverna* (tavérna)
τό τάβλι *backgammon* (távli)
τό τάληρο *five-drachma*
piece (táliro)
ΤΑΜΕΙΟΝ *CASH DESK*
(tamíon)
τό ταχυδρομείο *post office*
(tahithromío)
ΤΑΧΥΔΡΟΜΕΙΟΝ *POST*
OFFICE (tahithromíon)
τέσσερα *four (n)* (téssera)
τέσσερεις *four (m,f)*
(tésseris)
τεσσερεισήμιση *half past*
four (tesserisímisi)
η Τετάρτη *Wednesday*
(Tetárti)
τό τέταρτο i *quarter of a kilo*
ii *quarter of an hour*
(tétarto)
τέταρτο *fourth (floor,*
street) (tétarto)

Α Β Γ Δ Ε Ζ Η Θ Ι Κ Λ Μ Ν Ξ Ο Π Ρ Σ Τ Υ Φ Χ Ψ Ω
α β γ δ ε ζ η θ ι κ λ μ ν ξ ο π ρ σ τ υ φ χ ψ ω

τετρακόσια *four hundred* (tetrakósia)

τετρακόσιες *four hundred (drachmas)* (tetrakósies)

τό τζατζίκι *yoghurt and garlic salad* (tzatzíki)

τό τηλέφωνο *telephone* (tiléfono)

ΤΗΛΕΦΩΝΟΝ *TELEPHONE* (tiléfonon)

ΤΗΣ ΩΡΑΣ *FRESHLY COOKED DISHES (heading on menu)* (tis óras)

τί *what* (ti)

τίποτ 'άλλο; *anything else?* (tipot´állo)

τό *the (with n words)* (tó)

τό τόστ *toasted sandwich* (tóst)

τουριστική *tourist (class)* (tooristikí)

ΤΟΥΡΙΣΤΙΚΗ ΑΣΤΥΝΟΜΙΑ *TOURIST POLICE* (tooristikí astinomía)

τό τραίνο *train* (tréno)

η τράπεζα *bank* (trápeza)

τρείς *three (m,f)* (trís)

τρεισήμιση *half past three* (trisímisi)

τρία *three (n)* (tría)

τριακόσια *three hundred* (triakósia)

τριακόσιες *three hundred (drachmas)* (triakósies)

τριάντα *thirty* (triánda)

τριάντα πέντε *thirty five* (triánda pénde)

τό τρίκλινο *room with three beds* (tríklino)

η Τρίτη *Tuesday* (Tríti)

τρίτη *third (class)* (tríti)

τρίτο *third (street, floor)* (tríto)

τό τσάϊ *tea* (tsáï)

τό τυρί *cheese* (tirí)

η τυρόπιττα *cheese pie* (tirópitta)

τυροπιττάκια *small cheese pies* (tiropittákia)

Υ υ

υπάρχει *is there?, there is* (ipárhi)

ΥΠΕΡΑΓΟΡΑ *SUPERMARKET* (iperagorá)

ΥΠΟΓΕΙΟΝ *BASEMENT* (ipóyion)

υπογράψτε *sign (your name)* (ipográpste)

Φ φ

τό φαρμακείο *chemist's* (farmakío)

ΦΑΡΜΑΚΕΙΟΝ *CHEMIST'S* (farmakíon)

φάτε *(τί θά φάτε; what will you eat?)* (fáte)

ο Φεβρουάριος *February* (Fevrooários)

φέρνετε *(μάς/μού φέρνετε . . .;) bring us/me . . .* (férnete)

φέρτε *(φέρτε μας/μου . . . bring us/me . . .)* (férte)

η φέτα *goat's milk cheese* (féta)

φέτος *this year* (fétos)

φεύγει *leaves* (févgi)

ο Φλεβάρης *February* (Fleváris)

ο φούρνος *baker's* (foórnos)

τό φράγκο *one-drachma piece* (frángo)

φραπέ *iced coffee* (frapé)

τό φρούτο *fruit* (froóto)

ΦΡΟΥΤΑ *FRUIT (heading on menu)* (froóta)

φτάνει *arrives* (ftáni)

ΑΒΓΔΕΖΗΘΙΚΛΜΝΞΟΠΡΣΤΥΦΧΨΩ
αβγδεζηθικλμνξοπρστυφχψω

τό φτινόπωρο *autumn*
  (ftinóporo)
φωνάξτε *call, shout*
  (fonáxte)

Χ χ

χάθηκα *I'm lost* (háthika)
χαίρετε *hello, or goodbye
  (formal)* (hérete)
χαλάσω *(θέλω νά χαλάσω
  . . . I want to change. . .)*
  (haláso)
χαλάτε *do you
  change . . .?* (haláte)
χαρά *(μιά χαρά fine)* (hará)
ο χάρτης *map* (hártis)
ο χασάπης *butcher* (hasápis)
ο χειμώνας *winter* (himónas)
χίλια *one thousand* (hília)
χιλιάδες *thousands*
  (hiliádes)
τό χιλιάρικο *thousand-
  drachma note* (hiliáriko)
χίλιες *one thousand
  (drachmas)* (hílies)
χοιρινή *pork (cutlet)* (hiriní)
τό χοιρινό *pork* (hirinó)
τοῦ χρόνου *next year*
  (toó hrónoo)

τό χταποδάκι *octopus*
  (htapotháki)
ο χυμός *fruit juice* (himós)
η χωριάτικη *mixed salad*
  (horiátiki)
ΧΩΡΙΣ ΕΙΣΠΡΑΚΤΟΡΑ
  *ONE-MAN OPERATED
  BUS* (horís ispráktora)

Ψ ψ

τό ψάρι *fish* (psári)
η ψαροταβέρνα *fish
  restaurant* (psarotavérna)
η ψησταριά *restaurant
  specialising in grilled
  food* (psistariá)
ΨΗΤΑ *ROAST DISHES
  (heading on menu)*
  (psitá)
τό ψωμί *bread* (psomí)

Ω ω

ΩΘΗΣΑΤΕ *PUSH*
  (othísate)
η ώρα *hour, time* (óra)
ωραία *fine* (oréa)

Emergency

You can hear how to pronounce these words and phrases at the end of cassette 2, side 2

Be careful	**Προσοχή** Prosohí
Call a doctor	**Φωνάξτε ένα γιατρό** Fonáxte éna yatró
Do you speak English?	**Μιλάτε Αγγλικά;** Míláte Angliká?
Help	**Βοήθεια** Voíthia
I don't understand	**Δέν κατάλαβα** Then katálava
I'm lost	**Χάθηκα** Háthika
I've lost . . .	**Έχασα . . .** 'Ehasa . . .
Look out	**Πρόσεξε** Prósexe
Police	**Αστυνομία** Astinomía

ITINERARY	
DATE	PLACE

ITINERARY

DATE	PLACE

EXPENSES			
DATE	AMT.	U.S.$	FOR:

EXPENSES

DATE	AMT.	U.S.$	FOR:

EXPENSES			
DATE	AMT.	U.S.$	FOR:

EXPENSES			
DATE	AMT.	U.S. $	FOR:

PURCHASES

ITEM _____

WHERE BOUGHT _____

GIFT FOR _____COST_____U.S.$_____

ITEM _____

WHERE BOUGHT _____

GIFT FOR _____ COST_____U.S.$_____

ITEM _____

WHERE BOUGHT _____

GIFT FOR _____COST_____U.S.$_____

TEM _____

WHERE BOUGHT _____

GIFT FOR _____COST_____U.S.$_____

TEM _____

WHERE BOUGHT _____

GIFT FOR _____ COST_____U.S.$_____

PURCHASES

ITEM _____

WHERE BOUGHT _____

GIFT FOR _____COST_____U.S.$_____

ITEM _____

WHERE BOUGHT _____

GIFT FOR _____ COST_____U.S.$_____

ITEM _____

WHERE BOUGHT _____

GIFT FOR _____COST_____U.S.$_____

ITEM _____

WHERE BOUGHT _____

GIFT FOR _____ COST_____U.S.$_____

ITEM _____

WHERE BOUGHT _____

GIFT FOR _____ COST_____U.S.$_____

ADDRESSES

NAME _____

ADDRESS _____

_____ PHONE_____

NAME _____

ADDRESS _____

_____ PHONE_____

NAME _____

ADDRESS _____

_____ PHONE_____

NAME _____

ADDRESS _____

_____ PHONE_____

NAME _____

ADDRESS _____

_____ PHONE_____

ADDRESSES

NAME _____

ADDRESS _____

_____ PHONE _____

NAME _____

ADDRESS _____

_____ PHONE _____

NAME _____

ADDRESS _____

_____ PHONE _____

NAME _____

ADDRESS _____

_____ PHONE _____

NAME _____

ADDRESS _____

_____ PHONE _____

ADDRESSES

NAME _____

ADDRESS _____

_____ PHONE_____

NAME _____

ADDRESS _____

_____ PHONE_____

NAME _____

ADDRESS _____

_____ PHONE_____

NAME _____

ADDRESS _____

_____ PHONE_____

NAME _____

ADDRESS _____

_____ PHONE_____

ADDRESSES

NAME _____

ADDRESS_____

_____ PHONE_____

NAME _____

ADDRESS_____

_____ PHONE_____

NAME _____

ADDRESS_____

_____ PHONE_____

NAME _____

ADDRESS_____

_____ PHONE_____

NAME _____

ADDRESS_____

_____ PHONE_____

TRAVEL DIARY

DATE_____

DATE_____

DATE_____

DATE_____

DATE_____

DATE_____

DATE_____

TRAVEL DIARY

DATE_____

DATE_____

DATE_____

DATE_____

DATE_____

DATE_____

DATE_____

TRAVEL DIARY

DATE_____

DATE_____

DATE_____

DATE_____

DATE_____

DATE_____

DATE_____